THE TRADERS

THE
TRADERS

Sonny Kleinfield

Holt, Rinehart and Winston | New York

Library of Congress Cataloging in Publication Data
Kleinfield, Sonny.
The traders.
1. Floor traders (Finance)   I. Title.
HG4621.K53 1983   332.64   83-4383
ISBN: 0-03-059721-8

First Edition

Designer: Victoria Hartman
Printed in the United States of America
1 3 5 7 9 10 8 6 4 2

ISBN 0-03-059271-8

THE TRADERS

ONE

Finding space to breathe on the trading floor of the New York Stock Exchange is a continual worry. The floor is a scruffy, disheveled, high-ceilinged labyrinth that has the general appearance of a flea market. By now, a little after eleven A.M., it is already thrumming with excitement. A staggering crush of people dilly and dally around a maze of horseshoe-shaped kiosks where the major stocks of American industry get traded on a daily basis. Cathode-ray tubes slung above the posts display data and more data—the latest prices—in bright green letters and numbers. People keep staring at the screens as if they were playing video games. Crumpled wads of paper, soft-drink lids, husks of gum, and other detritus litter the grimy wooden floor. There is no room for wastebaskets, so there are none. Smoking is firmly forbidden on the trading floor, since one smoldering butt flipped into the snow of litter might quickly bring trading on America's mightiest exchange to a sudden standstill. Among other rules are grade-school–like prohibitions against running and playing radios. There's already enough noise. Intermittent high-decibel shrieks and howls constantly issue from far reaches of the room—calls to buy, calls to sell.

Unheeding of this rumpus, a man named Jim Connolly threads through the jam of bodies, his shoulders hunched forward. He steps briskly, then stops and casts an anxious glance at the tape up on the wall, actually a digital readout across which trades whoosh by at the rate of nine hundred characters per minute, a clip determined to be as fast as the human eye can read. He spots something interesting, decides to buy it, then, before shuffling off, vetoes that decision. He's not sure why. He shrugs and says with a mildly stoic look, "I change my mind about twenty times a day. It's the nature of the game." He peers quickly again at the tape, then slinks off merrily into the chattering, fidgeting crowd, secure in the knowledge that he will shortly find something else enticing to buy.

In good years, Connolly makes the kind of six-figure money that would allow him to work in a hushed office with a glorious view of the Manhattan skyline, a thick carpet, and a big desk carved out of mahogany. He could have one of those phones equipped with a maze of buttons. In fact, he enjoys no such niceties. His office is his pocket. If you need to reach him during the day, forget it. He has no phone. Connolly makes his living as a floor trader on the New York Stock Exchange, an occupation in which, on any given day, he might walk off the floor having racked up a small fortune or having blown one. The stock market is a shrine ostensibly consecrated to rounding up capital for companies to use to carry on their businesses. To Connolly, though, it is more like a high-stakes game of chance. Each trading post is like another gaming table, each stock another bet. You wander the floor, trying to decide where to risk your money.

Connolly is a big, husky man with the outward appearance of an English butler. He is forty-five. His light-brown hair is slicked back with hurricane-proof gobs of hair tonic, and he has a neatly coiffed mustache, which he tugs on every so often as if to make sure it's still there. He has a carefree manner, untrammeled enthusiasm, and a well-deserved reputation for garrulity. Like most traders, he also has a cocky assurance about him. This day, he is spiffily dressed in a chalk-striped gray suit and a sober blue tie (in contrast, the myriad brokers who wander the floor executing orders from the public and the big institutions are garbed in soiled, ill-fitting colored smocks that indicate the firms they're with). Pinned to the left lapel is a rectangular badge embellished with his name and No. 279 (everyone has a number on the floor), as well as green and red stripes, which signify that he is a floor trader. Connolly has seventeen years on the stock-exchange floor under his belt. This is his third year trading exclusively for himself.

As an independent floor trader, Connolly answers to no one. He risks only his own money. He doesn't have to worry about currying favor with customers; he has no customers. He doesn't have to concern himself with exacting performance quotas so that his boss will be impressed; he has no boss. He acts on a pure profit motive and lives by risk alone. "I'm an independent entrepreneur," Connolly will say when he is asked about his profession. "I'm a one-man company. I'm the factory, I'm the workers, I'm the whole shebang. There's only one guy I've got to please, and you're talking to him."

Much of Connolly's day can be described as that of a sort of professional scavenger, since he spends it perambulating around the floor snooping for bargains and pumping people for information that might lead him to bargains. In the course of most days, he buys and sells a bewildering array of stocks, avoiding putting too many irons in the same fires. He is equally comfortable owning an oil stock as he is owning a high-technology issue or an ant-spray concern. If he suspects that there's good money to be made buying into a disposable-crib manufacturer, he won't hesitate to take the plunge. There are 1,558 companies listed on the New York Stock Exchange, and when I ask Connolly how many stocks he trades in, he fishes in his pocket for some slips of paper, scans them quickly, then looks up. "This month is, what, five days old?" he says. "I've traded Telephone, Atlantic Richfield, Chrysler, Data Terminal Systems, Datapoint, General Electric, IBM, MLT, Mohawk Data Sciences, Teledyne (that's a hundred-and-twenty-three-dollar stock, one of the most expensive babies we've got down here; the typical stock goes for about forty bucks), Texaco, and Tosco. This morning, I traded in Amarada Hess. You can add that to the list. All in all, I would say I trade in fifty stocks a month."

As a rule, he rarely holds on to these stocks—he likes to call them "vehicles"—long enough to collect a dividend check. When his best judgment tells him to sell something, he doesn't shilly-shally around but simply washes his hands of it. Two or three days is almost an eternity for Connolly to be in a stock. Holding shares from eleven-thirty to two the same day could be considered long-term by his standards. Sometimes, he discovers two or three minutes after he bought a stock that he committed a boner in making the trade. (Traders call this errant situation being "long and wrong.") So he gets rid of it the first chance he has. A trader has to keep churning his money. Whereas a part-time investor can be satisfied to see paper profits pile up, the trader has to convert those paper profits regularly into cash to live on. Basically, traders like Connolly grovel for a tiny profit here, claw for another few bucks there. The returns from the transitory investments add up. As he explains it to me, "The economics of the trader are, we trade for very little increments. Eighths, quarters of a point. On an eighth of a dollar, we make money. On an eighth, we make about ten dollars. That's after clearing costs. The only costs we have are clearing costs and the cost of money. If you trade in the same day, as I usually do, there's no cost of money."

Grasping exactly how Connolly does what he does involves tangling with the inexplicable. As we trundle more or less aimlessly about the floor, struggling to evade being bulldozed by onrushing brokers and clerks, Connolly gives me as best he can a short course in his trading methodology: "A lot of traders tend to be group players, looking for the laggard in a group of stocks in the same industry, so that if a group is going down and one stock isn't yet going down, you short that one—in other words, sell shares you don't have in the hope of buying them later at a cheaper price. Or else traders tend to be excess traders. I do a lot of excess trading. If any household name, like Telephone or IBM, has some news come out about it, it tends to go up a disproportionate amount or down a disproportionate amount. Say IBM goes up a point. That's enough, and I will tend to short it. If Telephone goes down a point, I'll buy it. That's being an excess player. You feel the stock has moved an excess amount because of the public's emotion. If an oil company hits oil, the public overreacts, gets all excited; and the stock goes up. A trader would tend to short it. I mean, if an oil company didn't discover oil, it'd be out of business. It's not looking for wheelbarrows or hatpins. So the public tends to overreact. You get the announcement in which a company discloses a fire in one of its plants. Sure, it's a negative. But they probably have insurance and all, and so there will be more of a sell-off than there should be by the public. We try to take the emotion out of the game."

We cruise around some more at an easy pace, skirting a hairy-armed broker snorting something incoherent about the oils, and then Connolly pulls up, steals a quick glance up at the tape, and pats his stomach. "I trade mostly on gut feel," he says. "Trading is trading. It doesn't matter what I trade. I could trade orange juice and I could trade currencies—trading is trading. It's something you can't teach anyone. There are no graduate degrees in trading. I can take you around all day and I can't really tell you what I see up there that makes me trade. The one thing I can tell you: this is the kind of business where if you make a mistake your kids don't eat."

Some time ago, I became curious about professional floor traders—the small fraternity of hard-driving men (and handful of women) who make their living buying and selling stocks or options or pork-belly futures or wheat contracts. There is a class of people who don't like to take orders. They don't like sitting at desks and answering incessantly trilling phones. Back-patting and other distasteful rituals of office politics are not for them. They have exceedingly high opinions of themselves and they like to dream big dreams. They have an affinity for money. Money is their fix and rush, and traders often tend to be transformed into walking computer banks, humming with stories of fortunes made, fortunes lost. Presented with the opportunity to coin a plenitude of money quickly, traders are never timid about taking risks that, for most people, would send shivers through the bones. They look on themselves as men apart, financial daredevils who amount to the last individualists in America. If they aren't down at the gaming tables along the Las Vegas strip, such people trade for themselves on the floors of stock and commodity exchanges.

As I came to find out some elementary facts about traders, I decided I was drawn in particular not to the individuals who traded mainly for clients and who kept their pots boiling in large part from commissions, but to those who risked only their own money. Although I realized that even those who traded with the capital of their companies or their clients fell victim to the brutal pressures of performing well if they were going to keep their jobs, I suspected that the risks were not quite the same as when the trader had only the contents of his own wallet to ante up. As one trader was to tell me: "It's quite a sour taste to lose other people's money, but it's never the same as blowing your own dough." I was also not as intrigued by the group of individuals who traded for themselves out of their homes or from leased offices. They operated by scrunching before video-display screens that beamed the latest prices of whatever they were trading, and, when they sniffed a profit opportunity, grabbing the phone and calling a broker. It seemed to me that studying a green screen and yammering on the phone all day was an altogether less colorful way of trading than fending for oneself on an exchange floor.

The exact size of the army of independent floor traders is indeterminable, but it's been estimated by those in a position to know that there are at most a few thousand such individuals on the nation's exchanges. What fascinated me about them above all else were their footloose ways and their capacity for assuming awesome risks. Being someone whose stomach begins to heave upon chancing a niggardly ten-dollar bet on the shoo-in favorite in a Sunday football game, I was entranced by their deep sense of confidence, their per-

fervid belief in themselves. I wondered at the drive and te-
nacity that made traders stick with their profession despite
its dicey nature. Trading is not something for the diffident to
meddle with. If you can't abide pressure, I would often be
reminded, you don't belong in trading. Trading has almost
irresistible appeal, at least at first blush. It permits a person
to be his own boss and possibly to make gratifying sums of
money. When you've got a hot hand, trading can provide
indescribable thrills and all sorts of material and psychic
benefits. It is not that farfetched for a professional, in a blaze
of canny trades, to make a hundred thousand dollars in one
day. However, there are risks. It is also not that farfetched
for a blundering trader, or someone hit by a wicked slap of
fate, to lose all of a million dollars in a single jolting day and
not have the reserves to pay up. Seasoned traders, though,
can lose sums sufficient to launch a fair-sized shopping mall
and suffer no more than a spell of grouchiness, if that. Big
losses that they shrugged off are a topic that can absorb
traders for hours. So can the bliss of independence. I re-
called what a friend who did commission work on the floor of
the New York Stock Exchange but rarely mustered the cour-
age to throw the dice with his own money told me one night
over barroom drinks: "I've thought about this quite a bit, and
the fact is that nobody else today is his own man. Nobody
else is independent. Not Ronald Reagan, not the chairman of
AT&T, not the Ayatollah. But the trader can come and go as
he pleases and nobody's going to scold him. And he can
make as much money as he has talent. He's a very special
breed and I envy anyone with the guts to make it as an independent trader. It isn't something for the skittish, that's for
sure."

In pursuing floor traders, I was not so much curious about
ways to beat the markets or about the maddeningly complex

esoterica of statistical theory and probability that can be applied, invariably with mixed returns, to deciphering market trends (one could stuff a bookstore to bursting with the tangle of titles that purport to explain, in baby-talk language, secrets of obtaining riches in the markets; the people who really know how to hit it big, it seems to me, care little about illuminating ignoramuses but instead keep their secrets under their hats). Most of all, I wanted to know what the trader's life was like. I was interested in finding out something about what manner of individual was willing to engage in such a highly speculative field—where, according to the estimates of professionals, the bulk of traders go stone broke.

There are a few dozen exchanges—stock exchanges, option exchanges, futures exchanges—scattered around the country. The most prominent are situated in New York and Chicago, such institutions as the New York Stock Exchange, the American Stock Exchange, the Chicago Board of Trade, and the Chicago Mercantile Exchange. Over a period of some months, I determined to visit a few of them and to poke around and learn what a layman could of the trader's world. I'd heard that trading floors are somewhat like supermarkets, in the sense that various and voluminous products are available to trade, and different personalities gravitate toward different variants. Stocks are a slower-moving but quite capital-intensive game. Options seem best to allow the application of mathematical theory and the chance to hedge one's bets. Commodity futures, without question, are the fastest game of all and lure the really high rollers. Commodity traders, I had heard, were people who liked to swim with sharks. (Later I actually met a young New Yorker, a former free-lance writer, who fell into trading stock options after, in researching an article on the gold trade, he met a gold smuggler and developed big eyes. When he told me he was leaving for the Chicago commodity pits, I asked him why and he replied lightly, "I want to play with the man-eaters.") Anyone who traded successfully, though, was perforce exuberant, aggressive, opportunistic, unflappable, quick on his feet. "You can't be a boob and make it in this business," ran a cautionary remark I was to hear. So I set out to find and talk to and spend some time observing a core sampling of this ragtag breed to see what they were like and how they saw and practiced their odd and harrowing calling. Like the casinos along the strip in Las Vegas, the trading floor is a culture of connivers, dreamers, losers, and winners. It is a world of people yearning for the big score and sometimes getting it.

Connolly's working habitat is actually three rooms, one leading into the other: the Main Room, the Garage, and the Blue Room. No one knows for sure why the Garage is called the Garage, though there is a theory that it was added in 1922, about the time when the automobile was becoming a popular item and people were building garages onto their houses. The Blue Room, built in 1967, was named after the blue soundproofing placed on the walls. Immediate controversy surrounded it. Floor traders and brokers set store by the noise of trading; in the Blue Room, the recurrent din from the main floor is muffled. Some thought was given to installing a microphone in the Main Room and piping in the noise to the Blue Room, but nothing ever came of the notion. In all, the floor is thirty thousand square feet: the ceiling is a hundred and fifty feet high. A total of fourteen severely functional black trading posts dominate the rooms. It is at these posts that trading takes place. A trading post resembles Mission Control at a NASA space launch. Video monitors are suspended at clumsy angles overhead, dispensing price information in green lettering. Harried men cradle receivers and jabber on phones inside the post. Wires snake every which way. Litter piles up. Two hundred and fifty broker booths, where orders get phoned in for execution, ring the floor. All in all, some twenty-seven hundred people—the 1,366 members of the exchange plus their support staff and 700 exchange employees—congregate on the trading floor during the trading hours, 10:00 A.M. to 4:00 P.M., Monday through Friday.

The exchange, which is located in a gull-gray building at 11 Wall Street, is a nonprofit corporation which derives its income from members' dues and fees charged to corporations that list their shares on the exchange. Many people by now know its roots in the irregular auctions that were held in the late 1700s in a cramped room at 22 Wall Street. When the weather was pleasant, the brokers shuffled outdoors beneath a buttonwood tree before 68 Wall. (There's still a buttonwood tree outside the exchange entrance, gasping for life in the foul downtown air. The tree is periodically replaced, after the latest victim gives up.) On May 17, 1792, a contingent of twenty-four leading brokers met at Corre's Hotel and signed an agreement that created a securities market. That winter, the brokers put up a building at the corner of Wall and Water streets and called it the Tontine Coffee House, the forerunner of today's exchange.

On the floor coexist four subcategories of members. There are the commission brokers, who execute orders for clients of brokerage houses; the floor, or two-dollar, brokers, who help commission brokers carry out orders but work for no single brokerage firm (they used to be paid two bucks a trade); the specialists, who constitute the fulcrum through which all stocks are bought and sold; and the floor traders.

Connolly most often interacts with the specialists, who

busily work the outer perimeters of the trading posts, where they are easily accessible to brokers and traders. Some four hundred of them operate on the floor, enough to mind every listed stock, and most of them belong to firms with fat reserves; a typical specialist might traffic in anywhere from a half-dozen to two dozen issues, depending on how active he is. The stock exchange is basically an auction, and the specialist is the auctioneer, who quotes the bids and offers for his assigned stocks to the brokers and traders who come in search of a trade. He also acts as a trader on his own, using either his own or his firm's money. His basic charge is to keep the market in his stocks orderly and active. Buy and sell orders flow into his post, and they don't always match. Someone wants to buy Xerox at five points below the level at which it is trading, or to sell it at three points above. The specialist tries to balance out the orders, often by buying and selling for his own account shares that he does not especially want. Various authorities over the years have been trying to puzzle out a way to replace the specialist with machines, but so far without success. Each specialist maintains an orders-on-hand book, usually either a tawdry spiral notebook or a loose-leaf ledger of some sort, in which he keeps a record of all outstanding orders for his stock at differing price levels. When a bid or an offer comes in at other than the market price, it goes into the book, and if and when the price gets to that point, the specialist matches buyer and seller and executes the trade.

It takes a while to get the knack of what's going on on the floor. Newcomers are invariably bewildered, as I was, as to how order emerges from such apparent chaos, but somehow it does. When a trade is made (stocks trade in movements of an eighth of a dollar, or twelve and a half cents—not even enough to buy a newspaper), the execution is oral. Traders have a professional code. Like the rug business, trading is dependent on a man's word. Traders don't go back on their word. During the course of a trading day, they are often striking dozens of oral contracts. Sometimes traders realize almost instantly that they've made grave errors that will cost them a bundle. They don't renege. There are instances— and traders insist they are incredibly rare—when a trader won't honor a trade he knows he made. For all practical purposes, he is dead on the floor. He can't make a living anymore, for the reason that no one will trade with him. "A man stands by his word down here," Connolly says. "Been that way for a hundred and ninety years. Always gonna be that way." There's no queue or anything. You have to push or be pushed toward the specialist to get your order heard. If you're buying, you would shout something like "Three-eighths for a thousand," though if you're selling you would boom, "A thousand at three-eighths." "Sold" is said by a taker. The two parties hurriedly jot down the price and the number of shares on a slip of paper. Meanwhile, an exchange "reporter" records the same information and has it relayed to a clerk, who keys it into the apparatus that prints the transaction on the ticker tape.

His mustache wisping out to the sides, Connolly's eyes beat back and forth between the tape and where he is going. He once told me that he is able to recollect what virtually every stock crossing the tape had been trading at earlier that day, and thus is instantly aware of upward or downward trends. I check the tape myself, but my unschooled eye spots nothing that immediately invites me to plunk down some money, and so I ask Connolly what he's looking for. "I'll try to give you an idea," he replies with exaggerated patience. "The market is up, as they say, in a pretty good spike. I would be more likely to buy something than to sell it right now. So what I'm basically doing is looking for a clue that they're getting tired. By 'they' I mean the stocks. They will, after a while, get tired and start to come down. I'll give you a good example. Let's go over to IBM."

On our way there, Connolly bumps into a fellow floor trader with whom he is chummy and often plots strategy. After pumping his hand and engaging in some cheerful badinage, he informs him, "I banged out the Mohawk. It just wasn't working."

The other trader, masticating gum, squinches up his face and just nods, presumably not yet ready to bang out his own Mohawk.

As we push on, Connolly explains to me that he had bought some Mohawk Data Sciences, a computer stock, a few days ago, expecting it to advance because the entire computer group was in the doldrums and seemed due for some good action. His faith was misplaced. Nothing happened, so he got nudgy and sold the stock and swallowed a small loss. "I decided there were better places to put my money," he says. "You gotta get out of losers. The basic idea is to walk around this floor and not get too much blood on your feet."

We gingerly ease our way through a swarm of bodies and come before a video terminal and an owl-faced specialist that together represent the International Business Machines Corporation, behemoth of the computer world. The specialist looks a little down. Presumably suffering from a migraine, he sloshes some ice water on his face from a cup. After wetting himself down sufficiently, he blots his forehead with a handkerchief. As we stand there, a murmuring lot of brokers envelop him, continue to murmur but not to trade. Two men to my left are debating the prospects for the Jets, and two others are deep into a spirited discussion about mufflers.

"IBM sold at five this morning," Connolly says, meaning by this floor shorthand that it traded at sixty-five dollars. "The stock has been mildly positive. Not roaringly positive. And I was looking for signs that it was getting tired. That's obviously not the case, I see here. Some buyers took the shares offered at five. I'd expected it to get tired. If it did, I'd short it. So the jury is still out."

"Then you won't do anything?"

"No, I suppose not." He shrugs doubtfully. "You can always put your toe in the water: sell five hundred shares and see what happens. A famous trading cliché is, When in doubt, put them out. One premise that's been proven is that stocks go down faster than they go up. So to sell something short and see what happens is not such a big risk."

Connolly, unlike most of the public, doesn't believe everything is going to go up. When he suspects that a stock is ready for a nose dive he sells it short. In effect, he's selling something he doesn't own in the expectation of buying it back later at a lower price. This can be done because brokerage firms hold stock certificates in their own, or street, name, and loan it to the short-seller. Having to sell a stock short is the most perilous spot a trader can get himself into. The trader who buys a stock at a hundred dollars a share can lose only that hundred dollars plus clearing costs. The short-seller can have infinite losses if the issue keeps going up and up, though his gain is restricted to the price at which he sold the stock short. The effectiveness of the short sale has been hindered by the "uptick" rule, which says that a short sale can occur only at a price higher than the last different sale. If a stock, for example, has just traded at 39, 39¼, 39¼, and 39, both sales at 39¼ could be short (the last different sale being the original one at 39), but the last sale taking place at 39 could not. This removes the short-seller's ability to drive down the price of a stock through his own selling.

The chief reason Connolly can make money on razor-thin moves in a stock is because, unlike the public, he pays no brokerage commission. His sole expense on a trade is the fee he pays to the clearinghouse he uses, Spear, Leeds & Kellogg. Every trader must sign up with a clearinghouse, which in effect guarantees and processes his trades. On average, to make a round trade (buying and selling a hundred-share lot of stock), Connolly is charged $1.20. Sometimes, he will leave an order with a specialist to be executed when the market reaches a certain price, and for this he kicks in an extra commission. In terms of the money Connolly must put up to buy stock, he has no edge over other speculators. For stocks held overnight, he has to produce at least half the cash as margin, and for stocks bought and sold the same day a quarter of the price is necessary.

"Are there any other market sayings?" I ask Connolly.

"Oh, yeah," he says. "If the market goes down a lot for two or three weeks, the place gets very gloomy. One of the sayings then is, I'm sure they're going to turn because even the squad boys are shorting. In other words, even the clerks, the lowest echelon, have realized that the market is going down. If the market is booming toward the end of the day, it's said that you've got to have them for the opening, meaning you should take your stocks home overnight because they will probably open higher tomorrow. If it's getting sticky to sell, and you have to sell your stock in batches, and say you sold sixteen hundred of two thousand shares, then you say something like 'Four hundred at three-quarters, all the little old lady has.' It means you're not trying to go short but are just trying to close out a position."

Connolly booms a big laugh, as if he were hearing the expressions for the first time, and then clasps his hands in front of him and says, "Another great cliché is, I read *The New York Times* this morning and it cost me three thousand bucks. You read the front page today and the front page is bearish as hell—there's war and everything plastered all over it—and so if you came in bearish today you'd lose a bundle of money: the market is up three sixty-two. The point is, you can't have an opinion."

Certain stocks, Connolly says to me, have acquired floor nicknames. The Welbilt Corporation is affectionately referred to as Marilyn Monroe. Storage Technology (whose stock symbol is STK) is called Stickball. Hughes Tool is called Huge Tool. McDonald's goes by Hamburger. The Upjohn Company is known as Hard-on. The now defunct Pittsburgh Screw and Bolt was referred to as Love 'em and Leave 'em.

Even for a veteran like Connolly, trading holds an inordinate number of stresses and disappointments. Trading, one veteran told me, is like "driving a fast car on an oily road. You can be going good for a long while. Then, ugh!" Losing is certainly the hardest part of a trader's demanding line of work. Just learning to take a loss—any loss, however small—is, as trader after trader told me, the toughest thing to learn down on the floor. Losing money always casts a certain pall over Connolly's day, but the professional trader, if he's going to last, learns to live with adversity the way other people learn to live with a limp or bad teeth.

"You have to have a discipline down here to make it," Connolly says to me in the manner of a schoolmaster. "I have a hard and fast rule that I never let my losses on a trade exceed ten percent. Say I buy a ten-dollar stock. As soon as it goes to nine dollars, I must sell it and take the loss. Some guys have a five-percent rule. Some may have fifteen. I'm a ten man. The thing is, when you're right you're making eighths and quarters. So you can't take a loss of a point. The traders who get wiped out hope against hope. I've seen a good hundred come and go since I came down here in 1964. They're stubborn. They refuse to take losses."

Just about the worst jam to get into is to misjudge and then watch the stock simply cease trading, removing any opportunity for you to bail out. Some years ago, Connolly had eight thousand or ten thousand shares (the precise amount has mercifully disappeared from his memory) of the Dynamics Corporation of America. Far from showing any dynamism, the stock had been languishing for a while and he thought it was ready to bull its way up. His sense of smell was off. The company announced that it was broke, unable to pay its bills, and was ignobly filing for bankruptcy protection. The stock went into a tailspin. Trading halted, as a stampede of sell orders arrived. By the time Connolly was able to unload his holdings, he had dropped some twenty grand. It was one of the worst setbacks in his whole career. Connolly was a mite shaken, but that was about it. He didn't express any resentment or umbrage, but, rather, looked on what might have induced a seizure in someone else as more of a nuisance than anything to get upset about.

After hearing this tale of misery, I ask Connolly whether fits of mopiness or even downright despair ever overtake him during losing streaks. He smiles beatifically and says, "Everyone has his threshold of pain. I think my threshold of pain starts at about twenty-five thousand dollars. If I lose ten thousand dollars, that doesn't bother me. That's not uncommon in this business. You take ten-thousand-dollar losses all the time. It's like cutting your finger."

I look quizzical and say, "How can the disappearance of ten thousand dollars not bother you?"

"I have ice water for blood," he shoots back. "Every good trader has ice water for blood. If I were to make twenty thousand dollars in a day, I would do nothing different than if I lost twenty thousand dollars. If I have a date that night and I was going to go to a good restaurant and buy a hundred-and-twenty-dollar bottle of wine, I'd still do it. And I'd be just as chipper."

"What do you do if you hit a bad streak?"

"If you're trading one thousand shares, you cut down to five hundred. If that doesn't work, you cut down to three hundred. If that doesn't work, you leave."

"Leave?"

"Yeah, you just walk off the floor. On several occasions I've walked off the floor, gone home, and taken a cab out to Kennedy Airport with a passport and my American Express card and said I'll go anywhere I can get back from in ten days. I always keep a bag packed for that eventuality."

He fiddles in his pants pocket for a few seconds and extracts an Admiral's Club card, an American Express card, and an International Travel card and fans them out in his palm as if displaying stolen wares for sale. "That's all I need," he says.

Recent months (this was in the late spring of 1982) had been distinctly depressing for stock professionals; the sobering recession and high returns on no-risk investments had scared away the fickle public. Losses for the professionals during the previous winter had not been uncommon. "I took a lot of profitable long ski weekends," Connolly tells me with a certain smugness. "I would go away on Friday and come back on Wednesday and say I spent six hundred dollars and saved five thousand."

Besides the emotional horrors, there are physical ailments a trader has to worry about. Being in good shape helps. For one thing, you have to cover a lot of territory, and you can easily get footsore. Like traffic cops, traders are almost always on their feet. On any given day, Connolly figures he traverses five to seven miles. (Traders have on occasion lashed pedometers to their shoes to get precise readings of how much mileage they put on each day.) "It's not just the distance that wears you down, it's all the physical contact," Connolly explains. "You have to push and get pushed. People crawl all over you like ants. And the noise! As the market rises, so does the noise. It can get hairy."

Turning over inventory is important to traders. Connolly pushes out, or pulls in, roughly ten thousand shares a day out of the fifty or sixty million that change hands on the exchange (the record-volume day, set on November 4, 1982, was a staggering 149 million shares). How much he buys of a given stock depends primarily on its volatility and volume. A stock that trades big numbers—say a GM or an AT&T—Connolly will not be bashful about buying in sizable chunks, perhaps five thousand or ten thousand shares at a crack. However, with a "thin" stock—one that is not traded in great quantities, such as a Dow Jones—he will be far more conservative. It is said on the floor that an inactive stock "trades by appointment only." The brain of a trader registers volume and volatility patterns the way the brain of a golfer records pin placements and distances from fairway traps.

"You'd never trade twenty thousand shares at once?" I ask.

"Don't say never," Connolly exclaims. "I had twenty-seven thousand shares of Chrysler the other day."

"How come?"

"It looked right and it was. GM was acting very well. Ford was acting very well. Ford was up about two dollars. GM was up about three dollars. This is the laggard theory: Chrysler had to go up. I bought it at five and sold it off for eighths and quarters. It was a great trade."

Becoming a floor trader on the New York Stock Exchange entails a number of steps, all of which are fairly straightforward and dependent on one basic premise: having enough of a bank roll to purchase a seat. The term is really a misnomer, since a seat-owner rarely has any opportunity to sit down, and there are no chairs on the trading floor. The name carries over from the eighteenth century, when traders sat while the exchange president rattled off the list of securities for sale. The prevailing price in recent years has hovered in the vicinity of two hundred and fifty thousand dollars. In 1968 it touched a high of five hundred and fifteen thousand. In 1975, it sank to a piddling thirty-five thousand, and the gallows humor around the floor was that it cost more to own a taxi medallion than a seat on the New York Stock Exchange. Besides the money, a would-be trader must enlist the support of at least two current seat-owners willing to attest to his character. He must endure a credit check. Any criminal record unearthed is considered a blemish. Then he has to pass a written exam that certifies that he knows what a short sale is and what an uptick signifies. To make sure he's obeying the rules, the exchange requires that a trader submit daily reports of every transaction he makes on the floor. For some time, it was necessary for a trader to have at his disposal a nest egg of at least a quarter of a million dollars in order to venture onto the floor, though about a decade ago the exchange lightened the minimum to twenty-five thousand dollars in a largely unsuccessful campaign to woo new blood into the calling.

"You can't really do it on that small a stake," Connolly says over his shoulder as we briskly circle the floor. "I think you do need two hundred and fifty thousand to play down here. You realize how easy it is to spend two hundred and fifty thousand here? Go buy two thousand shares of General Motors. That's two hundred and twenty-five thousand. Go buy two thousand shares of IBM and you need a hundred and twenty thousand dollars. And two thousand shares is nothing. This is a capital-intensive business. I could take you around the floor and spend ten million dollars in three minutes."

In addition to the expense of his seat (a trader strapped for cash can also lease a seat from a member; the going rate in 1982 was between forty and sixty thousand a year), Connolly has to pay annual dues to the exchange and chip in to the gratuity fund for employees, as well as bear the costs of an accountant, a clerk, clearance fees, federal and state transfer taxes, and Securities and Exchange Commission filing fees. All told, Connolly figures these outlays run him about fifteen thousand a year.

It takes time, moreover, to solve the complexities of trading. Traders often do no better than break even their first year, if in fact they don't run a deficit. "When you first start out, it's extremely helpful to have generous parents," I was told by a trader who did have generous parents. Many lessons are painful. Skillful and wily traders will sucker you. Dishonest ones will try to cheat you. Some days, no matter what you do, nothing works. "You have to be resigned to the fact that some days you get your brains beaten in," Connolly told me.

Little love has been lost between regulators and the floor traders on the New York Stock Exchange. Over a period of several decades, the species has acquired a distinctly unsavory reputation with the SEC, the federal body that polices stock trading, which has waged a tenacious battle to put them squarely out of business. The nub of the Commission's objection is that traders boast a formidable edge over the public yet serve a questionable good. The suspicion, in short, is that they are earning big dollars by bloodying the public. Floor traders were not actually created for any specific purpose when exchanges came into being. It simply seemed natural to afford members the privilege of trading for themselves, if they saw fit. Those who did could pretty much do as they pleased, and celebrated big hitters like Jesse Livermore and Arthur Cutten could have a profound impact on stock prices. Only in later years, after the freewheeling and often abusive ways of traders came under scrutiny, were justifications for their existence formulated. The *raison d'être* of the floor trader, as commonly put forth, was to make the marketplace safer for the public by injecting liquidity, continuity, and stabilization. According to his defenders, the trader contributes "liquidity"—that is, makes it easier for people to buy and sell stocks of their choice—by virtue of being another individual engaged in active trading. "Continuity" of a market refers to the closeness of the prices of successive trades. It is better that a stock move in eighths of a point than in quarters or halves; otherwise, a person's position can deteriorate to an alarming extent before he can bail out of it. The presence of floor traders is said to increase the likelihood of transactions' proceeding in a narrow range. Traders are also said to impart "stability" to the market, putting a damper on prolonged downward or upward swings in stocks, because they often cover short sales during declining markets and they often trade against the prevailing trend of a market in a specific stock.

Myriad studies of the habits of floor traders, however, have cast considerable doubt on the soundness of these justifications. Traders actually tend to do most of their trading in the more active stocks, the ones that already enjoy great liquidity, continuity, and stability. After all, there is no money for traders in stocks that don't move or don't allow them to close out a position quickly. Also, studies show that traders, far more often than not, ride prevailing trends and therefore act not as stabilizing agents but as destabilizing forces. Starting in the 1930s, therefore, traders came under increasingly rigid regulations. Many of these were incorporated in the mighty Securities Exchange Act of 1934. An in-depth probe of the entire securities industry that was completed by the SEC in 1963, known as the Special Study of Securities Markets, called for the abolition of floor traders on the New York Stock Exchange, a cry that had been heard from the Congress and market critics for years. Among other things, the study declared: "Floor trading in its present form is a vestige of the former 'private club' character of stock exchanges and should not be permitted to continue. . . ." Arguing that floor traders did impart beneficial results, however marginal these might be, the NYSE refused to cave in, though it did lay down further restrictions on floor traders, cramping their style considerably and convincing many practitioners to abandon the calling. By the dictates of these rules as they now stand, Connolly and his kind must answer to an exchange official who summons them to help settle an order imbalance. A broker with a customer order in an inactive stock who wishes additional depth in the market can signal for as many as three traders. A floor trader also can't go short on a downtick. The public has priority over him when equivalent bids are made. And he must file with the exchange and the SEC reports on all his floor-trading transactions.

Whereas there used to be, as recently as a decade or so ago, some three hundred floor traders, no more than eight or ten remain active on the floor today (since 1977, when a new batch of rules took effect, they have been formally known as "registered competitive market makers" or RCMMs; there are also "competitive traders," at least half of whose trading must be public orders, making them quasi-brokers), and their combined trading accounts for something like .2 percent of New York Stock Exchange volume (contrasted with about 7 percent in the 1930s). The markets can still be sent reeling for a short time by the machinations of a big operator, but the days of cornering markets are pretty much gone. The heavy regulation has prompted many former floor people to set up off-the-floor offices and trade by phone, since the exchange has not yet clamped any restrictions on off-the-floor trading. Others have defected to the floors of options and commodities exchanges, where trading is still fast and footloose and new players regularly arrive to put up their chips.

"The individual trading stocks is dying," Connolly explained to me. "Everyone wants the security of being with a corporation. They want partners or something. In our society, trading floors are one of the last bastions for the individual."

The few remaining floor traders inveigh against the slew of

rules any chance they get. Connolly often feels that trading on the floor nowadays is like "working with one hand tied behind your back." For a short spell, he succumbed to trying off-the-floor trading. The regimen disagreed with him. "I think if you want to absolutely maximize every last dollar you go off the floor. But I like the floor. I enjoy the camaraderie of it, the kibbitzing, the bumping into people. I like the floor."

If Connolly tried to calculate his income on a daily, or even a weekly, basis, he believes he would undoubtedly "go absolutely nuts." Some days he would see a five-thousand- or maybe a ten-thousand-dollar loss. Other days he would be staring at a five-thousand-dollar profit. Still other days, he might make two bucks. How does one formulate a life-style? One day he would be sipping a marvelous Moët and the next day quaffing water. So he tries to look at things as if he were paid monthly. "Most guys like myself try to account in terms of months," he told me. "If you look back over a year, you may find you could make your whole year in two months. But the trick is, you don't know what those two months are when the year starts. You rarely make money every month. The way I figure it, you should make money seventy-five to eighty percent of the time."

When I asked him, Connolly said he guessed he winds up a loser on maybe 40 percent of his trades. The remaining 60 percent, however, are solid enough gains to constitute a healthy living. "If you're right fifty percent of the time, you're a winner," he said. "You don't usually lose more than two percent on a trade, and you make an average of four percent. Today, I lost a quarter of a point on Mohawk, a twelve-dollar stock. I lost a thousand bucks on a forty-eight-thousand-dollar investment. So I lost two percent on my money. Not so bad."

One of the aids of incalculable value Connolly gets from being on the floor is tips from brokers and specialists, which is why a trader cultivates peripheral hearing that enables him to overhear multiple conversations simultaneously. Traders are hungry for information, which is vital to their success. A shrewd trader learns to ingratiate himself with the other floor personnel—if not to butter them up blatantly, then at least to stay on their good side. A close rapport can produce countless gifts. For example, Connolly may have waltzed into a crowd at a post and decided to make a bid for five thousand shares of the stock, when a specialist glances his way and barks, "Jim, why don't you take a walk." The specialist is not being impolite. He knows that he has orders to sell, say, a hundred thousand shares of that stock, which are likely to drive down the price. So he protects Connolly. Without explicitly saying so, which is against the rules, he tells him to beat it. He may also obtain from brokers specific evaluations of investor sentiment, in terms of limit or stop orders to buy or sell a security when it hits a certain price, as well as in terms of short sales and orders canceled. These factors, not reflected on the tape, contribute to the "feel" of the market, which floor members cultivate. One way to gather intelligence is to read names—not personal names, but names of brokerage houses. In many instances, Connolly knows that a particular broker represents certain institutional investors, the mutual funds and insurance companies and bank trust departments that are the dominant factors in the market, and Connolly may monitor his activity closely as he begins to buy and sell large amounts of a stock. Floor people, though, will give away only so much, and only if they aren't hurt by what they divulge. Standing in the crowd at a trading post is not unlike sitting down to a game of poker: no one likes to give away his whole hand. "Nobody has enough money to play this game," Connolly often says. "You need help. If you don't need help today, you'll need it tomorrow."

While Connolly confers with a broker he's palsy with, I pause to watch a particularly boisterous stock specialist juggling orders.

"This market acts like cancer," he says scornfully. "Maybe worse."

He puts through an order. "Okay, sell it. Wham! Boom! Sold! Wham! Boom."

He picks up the phone, barks some rapid acknowledgments, gets off. "Okay, buy this stuff, buy it, buy it. Whoopee! Look at me! Look, I'm buying this stuff like water!"

He leans against the post and mops his brow with a blue handkerchief, emits a long sigh, and delivers a bilious stare. "Oh, you've got to be nuts to work in this business. Why am I in this fruitcake of a business? Does anyone know? C'mon. Line up and give me your answers."

I tiptoe away and go up to a nearby specialist I'll call Jerry Milton. (When I first met him, he made his position on anonymity abundantly clear: "No names. Not my name, not my firm's name, not the names of my stocks. Not one stock name, understand? Now, ask me anything.") Milton's appearance is clean-cut. He has a strong, deep voice and a jocose manner. Because he handles stocks that are not among the juiciest on the floor, he finds it necessary to do a considerable amount of trading for his own account in order to generate the kind of money that puts smiles on the faces of specialists. He tells me good-naturedly that he derives as much as 75 percent of his income from personal trading and only a quarter of it from commissions as a specialist. During the few hours I spent with him, I got the idea that investors were not exactly gung-ho about his particular securities. Nary an order came along. "I prefer running a book that way," he says, "because I'm trading-oriented. It's more exciting. It's more rewarding, because it's more of a challenge. It would be very easy to sit here on my rump all day and just write orders. Who needs that! I like to get up each day and play the game."

I ask the obligatory question: How do you decide when to make a trade?

"Through experience," he says, propping his foot up on a small fold-out seat screwed to his post. "Over the course of eighteen years as a specialist, I've had every type of experience—up market and down market, people getting shot, wars, you name it—and you learn how to react based on those experiences. I guess I've had everything happen, and I guess you store it in the computer in your head. You don't have a lot of time to decide, that's for sure. And you have to anticipate. You have to look at the tape and anticipate—two or three months, maybe a day or so, maybe two or three seconds before someone else. That's what makes you a good trader. The sound in this room plays a part in my thinking. The market is going down right now, but it's not a panic selling. It's just a steady drip, drip, drip, drip. If it was panic selling, I wouldn't be able to talk to you. I'd be so busy. If the market is up a lot, it's very noisy, too. People talk a lot about their bellies. I guess that has something to do with it, too. You do feel something in your gut."

He clears his throat with a loud harrumph and goes on: "You watch the tape. There's a talent to reading a tape. Later today, either the market is going to go further down or it's going to rally. It's down four fourteen now, at eleven-thirty. You have to anticipate when the rally will start and end. An outsider looks and sees the market down six points for the day. A student of the market looks at what the market was doing over the course of a day. Here, we live and die by that movement. The market is constantly breathing during the day. You have to breathe with it and sense its pulse. That determines whether you're a successful trader or an unsuccessful trader."

Do you ever hold on to a bad trade and hope for a rebound? I ask.

"Live in hope," Milton says ruefully, "and die in despair."

He goes on to say, "You try to stretch your profits and limit your losses. The worst thing you can do in this business is try to protect a bad trade. You do this and they carry you out of here. This reminds me of the kid who shits in bed and gets it all over his legs trying to kick it out of the crib. You see, a bad trade is like a diseased piece of meat. You don't want to eat any more of it. Throw it away. Bury it. Burn it. Just get the damned thing away from your mouth.

"When you're breaking in a new trader, the hardest thing to learn is to admit that you're wrong. It's a hard pill to swallow. You have to be man enough to admit to your peers that you're wrong and get out. Then you're alive and playing the game the next day."

A lot of traders don't learn that and fail.

"Oh, yeah." Milton nods. "There's a revolving door in this business. I've seen all kinds carried out the doors. The story is told that the tape never lies. The trend is your friend. If you try to buck the trend, they'll carry you out. If you detect a trend and you play it, you'll make a hell of a lot of money. If you try to pick the peak, you'll lose. They'll get the stretchers and carry you out. And the stretcher boys will be busy as long as God keeps making people with greed."

Connolly seems to be suffering from brain fag when I catch up with him again. He is staring meditatively at the tape. Nothing whizzing by seems to captivate him enough to make him part with any money. Somebody comes by and says he heard there was a Cabinet shake-up in Washington. Connolly just nods. To make sound trading decisions, a trader must weave a path through a thicket of rumors. The floor of an exchange practically explodes with information, the bulk of it innuendo, gossip, and outright deception. A small piece of it is fact. But, fact or fiction, information sends stocks up and down, and a trader has to know how to react to it. On December 3, 1981, for instance, a rumor from unidentified sources rippled across Wall Street reporting that President Reagan had been felled by a heart attack. Among other things, the rumor, despite vigorous denials by the White House, sent silver and gold prices sharply upward, and stock trading accelerated. There are always stories of deals that cannot miss. "I ignore all that junk," Connolly tells me. "I've never made money on rumors."

We are moseying over to the Blue Room to check out what's cooking when Connolly happens to glance up at the message board on one of the walls. It reads: "RCMMs Wanted at the Following Location: FGN 12A." "FGN" is the symbol of Flow General Inc., and 12A is the post at which it trades.

"Let's get over there," Connolly says.

When we arrive, there's a ragged crowd squeezed around the post and a blue light is pulsating on and off, another cue to floor traders that they should report there. There's a tremendous clacking of tongues.

Connolly plucks at the sleeve of a hawk-nosed broker he knows, catches his attention, and asks, "What's happening?"

"It's in the papers. The earnings were very disappointing."

The sour results have uncorked a torrent of sell orders, creating a glaring imbalance with the number of requests to buy Flow General, and so the specialist has been unable to open the stock for trading. He needs buy orders from the floor traders to even things up. Several other traders are already on hand, forking over bids. Connolly yanks out his sheaf of order slips and scribbles in a wobbly script an order for two thousand Flow General shares at whatever the stock opens at. He wriggles through the clump of brokers and hands his slip over to the specialist. Guesses are that the stock will start trading at around thirteen dollars a share. As he tramps off, I ask Connolly what Flow General does.

He shrugs. "I don't know, nor do I care. I may own the stock for fifteen minutes."

"Are you likely to lose money on the trade?"

"Yes," he rejoins right away. "It's part of the franchise."

"How often do you get involved in imbalances?" I ask.

"Some days, when there's big news, there are twenty of them," he says. "On Joe Granville Day [the infamous January 7, 1981, when Florida market seer Joe Granville advised his flock of sheep to sell every last stock they owned and the Dow Jones Average plummeted 23.80 on the then-record volume of 92.8 million shares], there were thirty of them.

On average, I'd say I get involved in twenty a month, almost one a day. I don't look forward to them, but trading isn't all honey."

Connolly slid into trading by accident. He was born in Brooklyn in 1937. His father was the treasurer of the Butterick Pattern Company; his financial acumen notwithstanding, he had no more than a feeble interest in the stock market and rarely dabbled in it. Connolly went off to Columbia College, where he settled into a pre-med program ("That was good training," he likes to say, "because there are a lot of sick people down here"). For reasons that remain hazy to him, he became captivated by the stock market and started monkeying with it at an age when most young men would be sinking their extra dollars into a set of wheels. Summers, Connolly drove a Carvel ice-cream truck along the North Shore of Long Island. He became locally renowned as the only Carvel merchant who stashed a *Wall Street Journal* in his truck. His ice-cream returns were the stake he used for his speculations. Connolly gets a reflective grin on his face when he recalls his first market plunge. The stock was New York Airways. "I liked the concept of a helicopter going to the airport. They subsequently went out of business, but I managed to buy at seven and got out at twelve." He responded to this good fortune with considerable alacrity. From then on, he had a pronounced stock-market bent. Unlike most greenhorn investors, he continued to win more often than he lost, and quickly became enchanted by how swiftly one's pile could rise. "I had to kill myself selling Carvel ice cream for seven hundred or a thousand dollars a summer, and I made four hundred bucks in a few days buying stocks. I mean, how could you not like stocks?"

The idea of healing patients understandably receded into the background. He came down to the exchange in 1959 and served a stint as an order clerk for Esterbrook & Company at a salary of $65 a week. He worked in an upstairs office, scribbling down orders that came in over the phone, a routine of often unmitigated drudgery. He showed enough talent that in December 1964 he became an Esterbrook floor broker. Three years later, he hooked up with another firm, New York Securities, where he stayed until he bought his own seat in 1972 for ninety thousand. He's been prowling the floor ever since. For a while, he had a joint-account arrangement with Spear, Leeds, under which the firm put up some chips for Connolly to bet in return for a split of the action. In 1979, he went entirely on his own. He is so fond of what he does that he sometimes thinks he is getting away with murder. As he likes to say, "I don't consider that I've worked a day in my life since I've been on the floor." When I asked him why he traded, he said, "When you're wrong you have nobody to blame. Plus I like doing things by myself. I think it's the greatest game in town."

Another floor trader I spoke to replied, when I inquired about the fruits of the calling, "I am a pure entrepreneur. I do what I like and nobody questions me and says, 'Hey, you buffoon, why did you buy three thousand shares of IBM? The market's falling.' I don't need to be told this. I made a mistake. I like to come and go when I please. I took off Friday. I took off yesterday. If the market doesn't feel right, I don't trade. If I have a sore toe, I want to be able to stay out and not have anybody question me: 'Now, just how sore is that toe?'"

Connolly is a bachelor. He lives in a stylish cooperative apartment at a good address on Manhattan's chic Upper East Side. One of the indulgences he allows himself is that he drives to work. No Mercedes or Porsche for him, though: a creaky 1971 Buick Riviera, two hundred and fifty thousand miles under its belt, is his preferred transportation. "It's a famous vehicle down here. I'm known for spending three hundred and fifty dollars a month to park a car that's worth two hundred and fifty." When the vintage of his car is questioned, Connolly's tart reply is: "It has zilch chance of getting stolen."

Typically, he arrives faithfully at the exchange at around twenty past nine. He takes the elevator upstairs to the Exchange Club, which is given the air of a hunting lodge by the collection of big-game heads that festoon the lobby walls. There he guzzles coffee at a leisurely tempo while holding pow-wows with fellow traders and brokers. He is looking for ideas on the strengths and weaknesses of various stocks. Who's tired? Who's ready for a rebound? Any takeover talk? Every morsel of information is sorted and then deposited in the appropriate bins in his brain. "I try to have a game plan," he says. "I want to be looking to buy 'em or looking to sell 'em." At around nine forty-five, Connolly picks himself up and moves down onto the floor to see whether today's game plan is any good. It's time to play.

Away from the floor, Connolly's two prime diversions are traveling and cooking. His penchant for distant lands is such that any time he spies an attractive package deal in the travel pages of the newspaper, he knocks off and hops aboard a plane. At cooking, he truly shines. In fact, he regularly rents himself out to perform the culinary work for private dinner parties. In lieu of a fee, he insists on a donation to the James F. Connolly Foundation, established to shower benevolence on worthy charities and hospitals of Connolly's picking. Two hundred dollars is what Connolly would consider an acceptable contribution for an eight-person feast (he once served forty and was handed a check for two thousand dollars). To rent Connolly, though, one must obey certain precepts. He must be reimbursed for what he buys, somebody else must undertake the dirty work of cleaning up after him, and he must, in all instances, be invited to join the good eating. Connolly's interest in cooking developed early on, and he picked up invaluable training by serving as steward of his fraternity at Columbia and as the mess sergeant of his National Guard unit. He would relieve unit members of ten bucks a weekend and in return would whip up dishes for them the likes of which few National Guardsmen have ever tasted.

As his own boss, Connolly is quite magnanimous with time off. "I would say most traders take six to eight weeks a year off," he remarked one day. "You take a lot of days off. Some mornings you come down here and at eleven you leave, because nothing's doing."

"Where do you go?" I asked.

"I go home."

"Go home and do what?"

Connolly smiled thinly and looked a little sheepish. "Well, actually, I have a stock-exchange tape at home that I rent for about a hundred and eighty dollars a month. I go home and sit and watch it. I'm addicted."

The tape rested against the wall in the corner, adjacent to a well-stuffed bookshelf. The apartment was a swirl of gadgets. A video camera sat atop a tripod near the entrance foyer. Some recording equipment was arrayed amid clutter on a desk. Perched on a Zenith console television was one of two videotape recorders Connolly owned. One of the cable channels broadcasts the New York Stock Exchange tape on a fifteen-minute delay. Whenever Connolly goes away for a long weekend or a week's vacation, he programs his recorder to tape the last two hours of trading on Friday. When he returns home on Sunday, he snaps it on and gets a sense of how the stocks have behaved so he knows what to do on Monday.

I sat on the couch. Connolly sat in an armchair with his feet propped up on an ottoman.

He had just returned from a soporific day at the exchange. The market had opened up and climbed steadily all day, a lousy pattern for a professional, who does his best in choppy, up-and-down markets. Connolly sipped a cool soda. Our conversation was interrupted by phone calls from friends whose interest, from what I could distill from Connolly's responses, centered chiefly on how the stocks had acted today. "Ah, they were the pits." "No, they stank up the whole room." "I should have stayed in bed and strung beads."

In between fielding calls, Connolly was telling me that an article of faith among floor traders was to close out your position on Friday. "There's an old Wall Street cliché: all wars and devaluations start on weekends. You don't want to lose money Sunday evening while watching television and have Dan Rather tell you about a war that erupted in Tripoli."

I pressed him on how much a stock trader can make. He smiled a minimal smile and got cagey. "Enough to live comfortably," he said. After some more arm-twisting, he finally acknowledged that it would be fair to say that successful ones made well into six figures. You have to earn good money if you're going to stick with such a chancy game, he said. "This is the kind of business where if you don't do well you starve. The scoreboard rings up every night."

I asked whether he thought of trading as gambling.

He grinned like a Cheshire cat. "Another cliché down here is that it's not gambling if you're winning."

He broke off and was silent for a few moments, then admitted that, as far as he could see, he didn't serve an especially vital economic function, but that it didn't bother him one bit. "I don't think in terms of my function," he said. "I think in terms of playing the game."

Traders basically subscribe to one of three broad schools of prognostication. There are fundamentalists, technicians (also known as "chartists"), and what might be called "seat-of-the-panters." Fundamentalists study up on the particulars of a company—its earnings, projected future earnings, management, the state of its businesses, its capital reserves, its debt, and anything else pertinent to its well-being. This dope can be gotten from the company's public reports or from summaries issued by statistical services such as Standard & Poor's. The technical school is much the opposite. Its god is prices. Its root belief is that the market automatically reflects everything about a company. All the good and bad morsels of information are already known to the people who buy and sell large blocks of stock, and so this information should show up in the price they're willing to pay or accept. "Discounted in advance," as Wall Streeters say. So there's no need to sweat over dull reports. Just look at the prices. To study pricing, technicians rely on charts—either of their own devising or bought from one of various chart services. In a fairly typical chart, a vertical line is used each day to record the price range of a stock, and a horizontal line to indicate its closing price. At the bottom of the chart, a second vertical line reveals the volume of shares traded that day. Then the chartist looks for patterns. Chart language embraces such abstruse phrases as "inverted bowl," "flag," "island," "dormant bottom," "wedge," "end run," "coil," "head and shoulders," and "neckline." Connolly doesn't believe in charts. He doesn't much believe in fundamentals. He goes by his instincts and feel for the market.

Traces of condescension, in fact, appear in Connolly when he is asked about market oracles and the cascades of stock letters, or tip sheets, that purport to lead their subscribers to untold wealth. Connolly sneers at any suggestion that the market is predictable or that anyone is endowed with market clairvoyance. "There's no greater reward than risking your own money and being right. These writers of stock letters obviously have no confidence in themselves. If anybody could predict the market, he would be doing what I'm doing. Joe Granville makes a million dollars or something selling a newsletter to fools, and he admits he trades no securities for himself. Most people regard the market as a part-time diversion. They get rewarded accordingly."

"You don't read any of those letters?" I inquired.

"I read them only for comic relief."

Connolly then hiked an arm back over his chair and told me about the "herd instinct."

"I'm Merrill Lynch and I'm a securities analyst and I'm going to recommend the utility stocks because I think the interest rates are going down. Now I'm Shearson. I can't afford not to recommend the utility stocks, in case Merrill's right. If we're all wrong, I'm okay, because how can people criticize everyone. It's job preservation. I call it the herd instinct."

"You would go against it?"

"Well, sometimes you can't go against the herd instinct. It can be pretty big. So you walk away and don't play."

The doorbell rang. Connolly's brother arrived. Connolly

introduced him and mentioned that he was a psychologist.

"That's what you need to figure out the stock market," Connolly said. "A shrink."

The trading floor: Connolly is all freshness and resilience when I catch up with him on a crisp fall day for another go at studying his habits. Trading has been fairly sluggish, so Connolly is sticking mostly with the active vehicles. He heads over to the GM post, where a half-dozen brokers are clustered around the specialist.

Connolly quickly digests the numbers on the green television screen and says with a nasal intonation, "A thousand at eight," thereby offering to sell a thousand GM shares to anyone who will pay him forty-eight dollars a share.

As it happens, Connolly owns no GM shares. "Why do you want to go short?" I ask.

"Because I think it's going down," he says.

"Why?"

"I don't know. I told you, there's no thought process involved."

Connolly repeats his offer several times, but there are no takers, so after a few more minutes he struts off. "If you can't do anything," he says, "you might as well go on to something else."

We make an excursion over to the IBM post. Earlier, Connolly had shorted five hundred shares at $77. The specialist reports that shares can be bought for 76¾.

"Take 'em," Connolly announces, covering his position at a nice profit.

After jotting down the trade, he says, "I probably made a hundred and fifteen dollars. There was probably ten dollars of expenses." He steals a glance at the ticker tape, then says,

"Let's take another look at Motors. Maybe we ought to be buying Motors."

We arrive at the GM post. Same story. Connolly says, "There really isn't anything to do. If there's nothing to do, you can't do anything."

Next, Connolly pays a return visit to IBM. Same story there, too. He is almost ready to leave when a broker arrives wanting to buy five thousand shares at 76¾. Connolly pushes into the crowd. "Five hundred, seven-eighths," he booms. A few more booms and the sale is made.

We stroll away and Connolly checks the tape. He sold some Warner Communications this morning at 39⅞ and notices a block of Warner crossing the tape now, inching higher. It dawns on him that this was a bad move. "It's going up. Nauseating."

He hustles over to Post 2, where Warner is traded. The stock is at 40⅛ and threatening a further advance. Connolly accepts the situation with seasoned stoicism.

"See, I'm losing. I'm always losing. If I get even, I'm going to quit."

After watching a bit with mounting gloom, Connolly bids: "An eighth, five hundred."

No takers.

"It's going up," he says to me. "It's going up."

"Three-eighths, five hundred" is his newly revised bid. A slope-shouldered broker grabs it.

"I'm wrong, so I covered," Connolly says. "I lost half a dollar. So I lost two hundred and fifty bucks."

"Are you upset?"

"Oh, God, no. You can't worry about it. This is how the market goes. Every so often it snarls a little and bites you. You'll get your chance to bite it back."

Many view the exchange as an anachronism that will,

sooner or later, be entirely replaced by a network of computers. The idea of an all-electronic exchange has been bandied about for many years, though the stock exchange has been reluctant to go that route. In May 1982, the Big Board finally got into the electronic swim when the first pilot test of the computer trading of stock got under way in a measly selection of just thirty stocks. Reviews were mixed. Exchange members who work on the floor mostly groused. After all, if the floor disappears, so do the men who walk around on it. So does Connolly. He is not perturbed. It is not a floor he needs so much as a marketplace. If computers do away with the floor, he expects he will trade from home, or trade in an office peopled by other professional traders, to retain at least a flavor of the camaraderie of the floor. "If prices are going to move up and down—and they're going to move up and down whether they're trading in a black box or a video tube or in a cardboard box—the professional trader will make money by picking the right stocks," he says. "You're not going to get rid of me."

"Let's go take a look at General Motors again," Connolly says now, and we return for the third time in a half-hour of trading to the world's biggest auto maker. GM is up an eighth since our last inspection. Connolly walks off.

Despite the lack of action, Connolly's desire to find trades stays on a high burner. He wants something, anything.

Where to go next? The tape bombards him with possibilities. AT&T? Digital Equipment? Ford? Procter & Gamble? Time Inc.?

Making up his mind as a squad boy speeds past, he walks haltingly toward Hamburger, the McDonald's post, shoots a glance at the TV screen, and then drifts into a leisurely chat with the specialist about a recent legal battle that had erupted between McDonald's and archrivals Burger King and Wendy's over Burger King assertions that consumers rate its burgers the yummiest.

"A McDonald's hamburger is a piece of shit," the specialist proclaims. He is a spindly man who looks as if he could use a few dozen Big Macs in his system.

"See," Connolly says to me, "he's short. If he's short, the hamburger is a piece of shit. If he's long, greatest taste in the world."

Connolly doesn't like what he sees at Hamburger, decides to make no bids or offers, and saunters back to Motors.

"Nothing," he says, with a sad shake of his head as soon as he arrives. "This is General Motors, one of the biggest companies in the world, and nothing. And I wouldn't mind selling some."

"What would you sell at?"

"I don't know," he says. "It's all a sense of feel."

There is a period of silence as he looks contemplatively at the TV screen. After a moment or two, he develops some feel and announces, "Five hundred at an eighth."

Silence.

"Five hundred at an eighth."

An order comes in from a brokerage house. Connolly sells his shares.

He shoves past a broker slouched against the wall in a half-autistic state. "Dead, Jimmy," he says. "You can't get locked up today."

"You're right," Connolly says. "Dead."

He descends anew on IBM. Nothing doing.

Raising his palm to his mouth to stifle a yawn, Connolly steps away from the post, nearly getting trampled by an onrushing clerk. He digs his hands into his pockets. He peers at the tape, the numbers and letters.

"You just keep watching," he says. "You keep watching."

TWO

Stanley Katz fishes some folded sheets of paper out of his inside jacket pocket, spreads them out in his left palm, and says to me that these are the key to his trading. The sheets, with a forest of numbers running across them, look something like the itemized phone bills of the world's most compulsive talker.

It is a morning in mid-April, rain is beating down outside, and I am near Post 8, deep in the recesses of the floor of the American Stock Exchange. Morning is the most optimistic time on any trading floor. Anything seems possible. There are few people about. Trading hasn't started yet, and so various traders are still huddled in the cafeteria, belting down coffee to get their adrenaline running. Littering the floor are crumpled buy and sell orders that presumably evaded brooms during yesterday's cleanup, an Orbit Gum wrapper, some pink low-cal sweetener packets, three rubber bands.

"You want to talk about trading?" Katz says to me, beaming a grin good enough for a toothpaste commercial. "You picked the right guy. I love to talk about trading. One thing you have to know right away, though. I don't trade the way most of the guys down here trade."

44

Katz takes himself and his methods seriously, and so I listen politely as he extols his own approach to amassing fortunes. Katz's game is stock options, but, as he explains to me, he pays no mind to indescribable rumblings in his stomach or fanciful whims or what the weather forecast is. Trained in statistics, he does what the numbers say. He has his own computer and a trading model that is plugged into it; and what his electronic master suggests, he does. From his perspective, trading is a multifaceted mathematical game in which stock options are the playing chips. "I'll play a hunch every now and then," Katz says. "But it'll be a calculated hunch." The system must work: I had been told by a number of traders that Katz possessed one of the hotter hands on the floor.

It's a cinch to find Katz. He is almost always lolling near Post 8, which he calls his "local pub," since he is rarely far from it and knows all the regulars there as intimately as saloon-mates at the neighborhood tavern. Post 8 is where the stock options of the Mesa Petroleum Company are traded. Katz's livelihood derives almost exclusively from the buying and selling of Mesa options.

Most traders on the floor of the Amex nimbly dart here, there, and everywhere during the course of a trading day, like prospectors trying every stream. Someone whispers that Procter & Gamble is soaring and they're off like the proverbial bat. Katz prefers not to be so restlessly nomadic. He stays put. Early on in his trading days, he established a *modus operandi* based on a personal fifteen-foot rule: he is not to trade any option that is transacted more than fifteen feet from his "pub." When he first fell into trading, Katz did hold positions in options that were a good hundred feet or so apart. He would breathlessly scuttle back and forth between the two posts, doing his best to keep track of what was doing at both of them. Things finally started to go askew. "I'm out of control," he told himself. "I believe in control, and here I am out of control." So he resolved that he was not going to budge more than fifteen feet from where his key option was handled, come bears or bulls.

As Katz is quick to explain to anyone who inquires about his methodology, "I don't like to give away money. I'm here to make money. If you're looking for money being given away, go talk to the tooth fairy."

"Hey, how's it going, Stanley?" barks a fellow trader—a big, bestubbled man wearing a sweatband around his neck. "You ready to make a killing?"

"Yeah, I sure am," Katz nonchalantly replies.

"Well," the trader shoots back, "where's your machine gun?"

"This is the mentality you have to put up with on this floor," Katz sighs.

Katz is decidedly good-natured. Like most traders, he has a king-sized ego. He is thirty-seven, of medium height, with lank dark hair barbered close to the scalp. His hair is combed neatly in place, and he doesn't look beaten down the way many traders do. He sees through gold-rimmed glasses. He has a thin, sharp-featured face and typically has a tense, ambitious look about him. When he is explaining something, he tends to gesticulate a lot. On the floor, he is usually clad in slacks and a beige sports coat; the coat is speckled with ink smears from pens that have misfired and badly needs the attentions of a dry cleaner. Pinned to the lapels of his jacket are two buttons; one says, "Happiness is being long puts," and the other says, "Chicken Little was right."

Katz has made his living trading stock options since 1977, always on the floor of the Amex, which itself only recently got into option action. Stock options existed as a trading instrument as far back as the seventeenth century in England; at that time they were known as "privileges." Americans have traded them for more than a century (first calling them "papers") on the over-the-counter market; however, volume was never heavy enough that someone could be confident of executing a trade when he wished to. What's more, early sellers of options to the public were not always the most upstanding individuals. Many of them frequently disowned contracts, giving options a sordid reputation. The Congress, in fact, came tantalizingly close to barring options when it passed the Securities Exchange Act in 1934. Even though it chose not to, organized options trading didn't spring into being until 1973, when the Chicago Board Options Exchange opened its doors and ushered in trading in a selection of sixteen stocks. The Amex lunged into the game two years later, as did some other exchanges (though not, as it happens, the New York Stock Exchange), and options volume now closely rivals that of regular securities.

Options seem baffling when you are first exposed to them. Simply put, an option is the right to buy or sell a hundred shares of a particular stock at a fixed price (called the "strike price" or "exercise price" in market lingo) before a set expiration date. The price paid for the option (which is physically nothing more than a confirmation on a broker's sheet) is called the "premium" and is always a fraction of what the stock itself would be trading at. It's established according to the volatility of the stock, the duration of the option, and the demand in the marketplace. In a typical instance, it might cost you five hundred dollars to buy an option on a hundred shares of a thirty-dollar stock. There are both "call" options and "put" options. A call gets the buyer the right to acquire the shares at the assigned price, which would typically be higher when the option is "written" than the price at which the stock is selling. A put gives him the right to sell the shares, and would be priced below what the stock was going for. A buyer of calls is betting that the underlying stock is going to rise in price. Say you paid five dollars a share for a call option to buy Continental Trash at thirty-five dollars sometime in the next sixty days. Continental Trash is currently trading at thirty dollars. Two months later, though, it's going for fifty dollars. You could exercise your option and buy the stock at thirty-five a share from whoever issued the call and then turn around and sell it at fifty. Thus you paid thirty-five dollars plus the five dollars a share for the call option, netting you ten dollars a share, minus brokerage commissions (something a floor trader avoids). A put buyer, on the other hand, is betting on a collapse in the stock price. If you bought a put option with a strike price of twenty-five dollars and Continental Trash slipped to twenty dollars, you would exercise the option and sell the shares at twenty-five to an issuer of the put and then go buy the stock on the open market at twenty, producing a profit of five dollars before commissions.

Options expire at three-month intervals; nine months is the lengthiest regular expiration period. As a general rule, options rise and fall in value in tandem with swings in the underlying stock, though myriad factors can cause them to slip out of line, and when they do, profit opportunities crop up for traders. To delve into some more market parlance, a call option is said to be "in the money" when the market price of the stock is higher than the call's strike price (the opposite is true for a put option). It is "out of the money" when the stock price is lower than the strike price, and it is said to be "at parity" when the option price plus strike price are equal to the stock price. So it is not uncommon to see traders dragging their feet and grumbling about when are they going to get in the money already, and about how they've been saddled with all of these out-of-the-moneys. A big appeal of options is the leverage they provide: you pay much less for an option than you do for the stock itself, and if you're wrong and your option expires worthless, you can't lose any more than what you paid for it. Stocks, moreover, offer few investment possibilities—you either buy them or sell them. But the game of options trading embraces all manner of arcane techniques that enable a trader to cut his risk, since there are puts and calls with different strike prices and more than one duration. A common technique is the spread. In theory, there should be a neat relationship between the prices of options in ensuing months (or varying strike prices in the same month) in any given stock. A later month's price should exceed an earlier month's by the expected movement of the underlying stock. In practice, however, differentials do get out of whack at times. This makes it appealing to "put on" spreads, or "straddle," simultaneously going long in one month and short in another. When the values fall back into line, the trader sells the spread at a profit. His risk is lowered because he doesn't have to be right on what happens with both "legs" of the spread. Traders taking a spread position don't care about upward or downward price movement, either, since the profitability of a spread is determined by changes in the difference (or spread) between the prices of the two contracts.

Spreads are also a darling among traders because they enable them to fashion artificial tax losses and thus pay piddling income tax on often gargantuan earnings. What a trader does is liquidate losing legs of a straddle to create short-term losses to shelter gains, keeping the winning legs (taxes on which he defers until he liquidates them) and keeps rolling his money over into new straddles until, as it's said on the floor, he has deferred taxes to the point where he "pays from the grave." As I came to find out, there are myriad types of spreads that the trader can pull out of his bag of tricks. There is, for example, the "time spread," in which the strike prices of the options are identical but one option lapses much sooner than the other. There is the "sandwich spread," made up of four or more calls at three different strike prices—a long call is at the highest price, with another long call at a low price, and then two short calls positioned in between. There are the highly risky "naked calls," when a trader sells an option without owning the underlying stock or any other options as protection. (When a trader does own the stock or another option, then he has a "covered call.") There's the "strap," a combination of two calls and a put. There's the "strip," which involves two puts and a call. And so on.

Out of this grab bag of possibilities, traders pluck their own favorite stratagems. Katz's dish, he explained to me one afternoon, is "volatility spreading"—trading options of stocks whose prices gyrate enormously. "For me to be interested in something, it first of all has to have a lot of public interest in it. That means there will be orders on the books to buy and sell. It means you'll be able to do volume. It also means the stock will move. Then I want stocks that have a history of inconsistency. That is very important because otherwise everyone after a while knows what everything's worth. I need the inconsistency to have profit opportunities. The inconsistency tells you that different options at different times are underpriced or overpriced."

The American Stock Exchange inhabits a fairly bland-looking gray building at 86 Trinity Place, adjacent to New York University's Graduate School of Business Administration. Presumably, under ideal circumstances, students can pick up their degree in statistics or economic theory, saunter out the door, make an abrupt right, and march onto the Amex floor, there to put theory promptly into practice. To your right as you enter the Amex building is the members' lounge, a small and somewhat ratty chamber that contains a chattering Dow Jones ticker against the far wall, battered stand-up bookshelves crammed with Standard & Poor's stock directories, paintings on the wall depicting the exchange's formative days, several soiled couches and easy chairs, and, more often than not before the day's trading begins, several slumbering traders. (The conversation among those who are conscious is not always directly related to the price movements of particular issues. Sitting in the room one day awaiting the arrival of a tardy trader, I heard a broker inform another, "This guy is a Cadillac among paper-hangers. He can hang paper like nobody's business." "Yeah, but does he do Levolors?") Down a flight of stairs is the locker room, where the floor personnel shuck their suit coats and shrug into colored smocks. Cubbyholes hug the wall, into which traders and other floor personnel stuff their hard-soled Florsheims and Bally street shoes, to slip into soft-bottomed trading shoes.

The trading floor itself, which is up a short flight of stairs from the members' lounge, is essentially a giant square, stretching about a hundred and fifty feet on each side. Twenty octagonal trading posts are spaced about the floor, and three tiers of booths ascend bleacherlike along three sides of the floor, the headquarters of the clerks who work for the brokerage houses.

The Amex originally conducted its dealings outdoors. The precise year when the exchange sprang into being has been lost in antiquity, though historians generally pinpoint its birth as being somewhere between the Gold Rush of 1849 and the outbreak of the Civil War. Until 1953, the exchange was known as the Curb Exchange, an allusion to its outdoor origins. Presumably spawned by a collection of virile brokers unenthusiastic about the indoor life then being offered by the New York Exchange, the outdoor marketplace was an almost laughably informal, highly unpredictable place of business. It was not necessary to purchase a seat to join in the action. You wanted to trade stocks? You had only to come on down and start soliciting orders. You convinced clients not on the basis of your history of savvy brokerage or by the bulk of your capital base, but by your immediate charm and salesmanship. Lung power had something to do with your effectiveness as a trader. The arena was shifted several times, but it attained its height of activity along Broad Street. Brokers totally overran the artery, making traffic movement impossible. When cars attempted to wend through the street, husky traders occasionally applied their brawn to front bumpers and sent them rolling backward. As trades took place down on the street, telephone clerks perched in the windows of the buildings that fronted on Broad Street, wearing headsets that connected them with brokerage houses. They communicated with the traders, who donned gaily colored hats to make themselves more quickly recognizable to their clerks, by way of hand signals. According to historians, it was not unknown for an overexcited messenger, perhaps on landing a gigantic order, to lose his balance and tumble down to the street. It was a hale and hearty lot that traded. The men were known to favor a drink or ten, and were not bashful about busting a fellow trader in the jaw if a transaction turned out to be unsatisfactory. In 1908, the market advanced toward organization when a cadre of brokers formed the New York Curb Agency, and in March 1921, the exchange finally moved indoors, though some dissident traders persisted in conducting their activities in the open air for some time afterward.

On the dot of ten o'clock, an Amex functionary officiously raps the gong with a small hammer to open trading. A hollow-eyed trader standing to my immediate left fidgets ever so slightly and declares, "In all my years here, I've never gotten used to that gong. It still scares me." Stanley Katz is comfortably settled at his local pub, nibbling at his nails, one knee canted out. His eyes swivel nervously up and down, up to study the shimmering video terminals reporting the option activity, down to peer at his computer sheets. Katz trades predominantly two options—Mesa and Tandy, an electronics company best known among the public for its Radio Shack retail outlets—both, of course, spaced within fifteen feet of each other. It often seems as if he trades just one, since much of the time he stays at Mesa. "I got into Mesa in the summer of 1978, when there were takeover rumors and the stock was moving a lot," he says to me. "I got in there to fool around a little and I liked it. What can I say? Mesa's been good to me, and you don't get off a winning horse."

Mesa Petroleum is an oil and gas explorer and producer. Founded in 1964, it drills in the United States, Western Canada, and the North Sea. In 1982, it had revenues of some 407 million dollars. It is based at One Mesa Square in Amarillo, Texas. Quite possibly I have already recited more about Mesa Petroleum than Katz knows. He sees no need to know a great deal about it. Brass tacks about the company really don't figure into his trading decisions. For the most part, he's curious about past price swings and what they portend. Little though he may know, Stanley Katz is as reliant on Mesa Petroleum for his subsistence as is T. Boone Pickens, Jr., the president and chairman of the board of Mesa.

At home, Katz keeps an IBM home computer. Tucked within its memory is the Black-Scholes options model, an ingenious conception, made public in early 1973, of Fisher Black and Morton Scholes, professors of economics, which predicts options values using an equation into which are plugged several variants, most notably the stock price, the strike price, the time remaining until expiration, the current interest rate of risk-free investments, and the volatility. The formula is fairly easy to use and has attracted a goodly number of believers, besides inspiring assorted imitations. Each night, Katz types in the crucial elements of the day's trading session and, in the space of about twenty minutes, his IBM quietly churns out two small sheets of numbers, one sheet for each of his two options, reporting the fair value of the options for each price of the stock at half-point intervals. From these numbers, Katz deduces when an option is underpriced and when it is overpriced. "I don't believe in numbers," he says. "What I believe in is patterns. The individual numbers themselves mean very little to me. What I do is, I circle something when I buy or sell it, and I sort of keep track of these. Over the course of a day those things start to form patterns."

What's a useful pattern? I ask.

"Anything that doesn't represent a vertical line," he says at once. "A vertical line means they're all priced in accordance with the stock, meaning they're neither undervalued nor overvalued, and so I should close out my position. My strategy is to buy undervalued and sell overvalued options. So anything but a vertical line represents a profit opportunity. The further away from the vertical position the pattern gets, the more opportunity and the more trading I'll do."

Katz is giving grave attention to his sheets, seeking to pry loose the market's secrets. Clutching them in the palm of his left hand, he unfolds them just enough to sneak a peak at the numbers, then neatly folds them back up and returns his gaze to the flickering tubes. His eyes slide over the numbers. He taps his right foot. He reminds me of the college undergraduate whose method of taking an exam includes reliance on crib sheets. There is, of course, nothing at all irregular or unethical about seeking help from computer printouts, though, in this regard, Katz is party to a small, albeit growing, contingent of scientific traders. Those who trade according to telltale movements in their bellies will at times regard the ways of the computer men as something of a breach of taste. "There's a natural amount of resentment by some of the older traders," Katz tells me. "It's partly a function of age. We're stepping on their toes to some extent. These people grew up with the notion that trading is almost an art form, and doesn't require mathematical knowledge and familiarity with statistics. It was done with gut feeling. If you have natural talent and somebody comes along and has less natural ability but has the ability to analyze and does as well as you do, that breeds resentment. So you might go into a crowd with a chart and there'll be a bid and you won't go for it and one of the guys will say, 'Hey, what's the matter, buddy, your charts say you can't do that? What's the matter? You can't do anything unless your sheets say so?'"

Katz—who will trade six hundred to eight hundred option contracts in a heavy-volume day, when buy and sell orders seem to stream in like an undammed river, and as many as two hundred to three hundred even when the exchange is relatively sleepy—trades four Mesa puts now, bellowing out "Sold" when a broker shouts an offer. Katz gets a price that at once brings him earnings of several hundred dollars— money that has rolled in just since three-thirty yesterday because of a rise in the price. It is now approaching eleven o'clock. To Katz, however, these are just modest crumbs.

"This is just nickel-and-dime stuff," he remarks. "I'm just day trading, taking offers, making bids, in order to help make the market, to keep it liquid. There are quite a number of traders down here who make a hell of a lot of money doing nickel-and-dime stuff like this, just trading all the time. I believe in positions that I don't turn over for a couple of weeks. That's where I make my real money."

As with stocks, options trading on the Amex is umpired by specialists, who match up buy and sell orders as well as trade for themselves, to keep an orderly market. Under exchange regulations, floor traders are supposed to shout out any bid so that the specialist hears it and has an opportunity to participate in the trade, one reason being that if there are public orders on his book these get executed first. In actuality, during a volatile market, when a pack of traders mob a post, traders will at times end up haggling just among themselves, without the specialists' knowledge, a practice known in the lingo of the floor as "trading on the perimeter."

Unlike stock traders, options traders don't wear the albatross of heavy regulation around their necks. They can pretty much trade with the same abandon as a member of the public, and though there is a stipulation that allows them to be brought in unwillingly to help settle an unstable market by making an unprofitable deal, it is rarely enforced. Consequently, far from being a dwindling species, options traders who trade for their own accounts are an active and growing coterie. The Mesa post is regularly populated by a half-dozen and sometimes as many as fifteen or so independent traders clamoring for action.

Katz massages the part of his forehead between his eyebrows, as if he has a splitting headache. He massages his left shoulder. He massages his right shoulder. He suppresses a yawn. His neck cranes upward, as if he were checking for rain. He brushes some lint off his jacket, which has acquired several additional ink smears.

A dozen or so traders are packed chockablock around the Mesa post, eyeing the movement of the options, anxiously waiting for orders from floor brokers to pour in. Kibbitzing, just passing the time. One man is entirely bald, one man has probably not seen a barber since the last great bull market, another trader is of a girth that suggests there have always been bull markets. There is a steady patter of conversation. "The Julys just aren't doing a damn thing." "How about those Octobers? You see where those Octobers are going?" "They're going down a drainpipe." "They're going to hell in a handbasket."

One trader threatens, for no apparent reason, to shove a Reddi-Whip can down the nose of another orange-smocked trader. "I tell you, you'll like it," he swears. "It's a real high. I'll bet half of the guys here are on Reddi-Whip."

A buy order is now ordered. The traders pounce. Raw meat thrown to the lions. There's an appalling racket.

"July seventies. Five-eighths for twenty."

"Hey, Bobby, how are April thirties?"

"Bobby, I need some July thirties."

"Sell two, Bobby. C'mon, I'll sell two."

"Hey, how are the July thirties?"

Traders and brokers repeatedly inquire about the price of an option in the way that hospital visitors might ask after the health of an ailing in-law—how is this one, how is that one. The answers they are looking for are not framed in terms of heartbeat or blood pressure, but telltale prices, what is up and what is down. "How am I doing?" is basically what they're asking.

"This business is like fording a river by jumping from one slippery rock to the next," a trader informs me darkly. "You're always concerned about drowning."

Each trading post is its own principality, embodying its own blend of trading characteristics. To a large extent, these have to do with traits of the stock represented at the post, but they also have to do with the personalities of the traders who most often mingle there. Post 8 is known as one of the friendlier places to trade. As one regular patron puts it, "This is where all the nuts are assembled in one place." There is an amity among the traders, and the specialists there are personable and convivial. They appreciate the traders in the crowd. Some specialists are hoggish. They want all the profits for themselves. If they can, they'll stick traders with bad deals. Katz abandoned trading at one post in disgust, even though he was doing fairly well there, because of the caustic attitude of the specialist. "He was a real pig," Katz recalls. "He would deliberately cut you out. He didn't want traders. Personally, I think he'd have more liquidity if he had a lot of traders in the crowd. But he discourages traders, and I think in the long run he discourages the public."

Some Mesa puts sound good to Katz, and so he takes five. Sells four calls. Buys two July puts. Checks his computer sheets. Breathes out relief.

"A good stock trader can make an awful lot of money," he comments between trades, "but he has to be right fifty-five to sixty percent of the time to make substantial money. An options trader has the ability to hedge his bets—he can buy the underlying stock and do all sorts of combinations—and so he probably only has to be right forty-five to fifty percent of the time to make big money. He's already on the side of the angels. A scientific trader like myself, I find from going

over my figures, only has to be right about thirty-five percent of the time. That's because I don't usually have stock
positions, so if the stock goes up or down a point, I don't give
a damn."

As we talk, Katz happens to glance at the Mesa screen,
and a frown crinkles his face, as if he has just learned he has a
malignant tumor. "Jesus, things are collapsing today. I'll
probably lose a little bit of money." He does some mental
arithmetic and shrugs his shoulders. "Well, I'll get it back if
the market moves."

"The range of income down here is staggering," Katz says
several afternoons later, when the market is on the drowsy
side. "There are guys down on the floor who just make an
okay living and there are other guys who make veritable fortunes. Some options traders make twenty thousand dollars
or thirty thousand dollars a year. Others make a million
bucks. In 1980, which was a very big year for the market—
the volume was just tremendous—good traders made two
hundred and fifty thousand to a half a million dollars. Volume just exploded, and some people were doubling and trip-
ling their income." I hear about a young woman trader who,
in her maiden year on the floor, cleared only five thousand
dollars and must have wondered about pursuing her original
career objective, that of a librarian, but she rebounded to
around ten thousand the second year and then, in 1980,
racked up a neat hundred and five thousand dollars and
surely put aside stacking books for good.

Options, though, with their leverage, can enrich or im-
poverish a trader at blazing speed. "People's positions can
swing from day to day by a hundred thousand dollars," Katz
explains to me when I ask him about such a tipsy existence.

"My position, on average, will swing forty thousand dollars from day to day. I have pretty consistent month-to-month profits, however. I will probably make money ten months out of the year and lose during two. You have to make money in the heavy-volume months or you're not going to come out too well in this game. I know some people with unbelievable records. I know people who have never had a losing month down here, or never had a losing week. Or so they maintain."

How do you shake the miseries of losing days? I ask Katz.

"I don't know if you ever learn to deal with it," he says. "You learn to cope with it as a means of self-defense. Sometimes you feel you have no control, and you say, Okay, I'm going to take all my losses and start fresh. Now, my risk is not so great compared to my capital. I don't have the fear that I'm going to be wiped out that I had at the beginning. When you have thirty thousand dollars' worth of capital and you could lose fifteen thousand on the opening—I mean, that's fear. That's shaking-at-the-knees fear. I worried a lot back then; now, it's more annoyance than fear. I mean, no matter how much you have, nobody likes to lose money."

Since he has such an analytical nature, I put to Katz the question of who excels at trading, and he says, "One type is the person who is well disciplined. There is another person who may not be well disciplined who can excel because he has the street instincts to know when to get out of a losing position. The person who won't excel is someone with no self-confidence. You have to have self-confidence. If you don't, you'll never let a good position run. You'll get stubborn. There are people on the floor who are overconfident, but they're good traders because they're not stubborn. It can be bad to be very emotional, but it's more lack of discipline that hurts. There's a famous story on the floor of Ron Rose, the old double-up. He was naked short during a period a few years ago when the market roared upward. Instead of covering, he doubled his position. He supposedly lost something in the area of eight hundred thousand dollars and was wiped out. That's a lack of discipline. For several Christmases guys on the floor used to give out the Ron Rose Memorial Award to the trader most likely to go bankrupt." Ron Rose, I hear from another trader, was last spied peddling sweaters in the garment district.

Losses don't rattle traders so much as an inadequacy of funds with which to bet on future winners. There are traders who have so often wobbled on the edge of the abyss, only to waltz away, that they are said to have more lives than a cat. I was on the Amex floor one time when a trader of about twenty-seven came up to me and, with a small prefatory cough, suggested a cup of coffee in the members' cafeteria. His name, he said, was Michael Moss. He was lankily built and wore his hair cropped short, and he looked to me like some up-and-coming management trainee fresh out of a Dale Carnegie course. The cafeteria was on the dumpy side but well populated. Sipping coffee and talking losses, Moss said, "My father [a retired but solvent trader] told me that the greatest sin on Wall Street is to go broke. You've got to keep the doors open. You have to keep playing."

Moss graduated from Lehigh University with a marketing degree. He admitted that he did not have a head for hard work. When he interviewed at some ad agencies, he was advised to return to school for an MBA. Moss said forget it, called his father, and got a clerk's job on Wall Street. He quickly developed a consuming passion for the business. A couple of years later he was a broker, and a couple of years after that he was a trader.

"I love the business," he said. "I'm a prospector. I'm always willing to put up money to make a little bit of money. I like the freedom. I have my own ship. There are no office politics. My destiny is my own. It's my ballgame. I can play any way I want. I can bunt, I can go up the middle, I can swing for the fences."

He gave a hard laugh. "There are some guys who have these big egos. They have to take the risks. I'm running the market, is their attitude. I'm smarter. I can outguess the market. Those are the swingers."

More coffee went down, and he continued: "The excesses of the business are where the stories come from. The players. They bet the ranch. They bet the franchise. I couldn't do it—get up to the plate and lay it all on the line. But I'll last. I won't go bust. Plus, there's something wrong with making money too fast. Making a million or two million smackers from nothing! There's something wrong with that, in my book."

"I presume you have made no fast money," I remarked.

"Well, in January 1980 I started my account with twenty-five thousand dollars and made a pinch under four hundred thousand that year. Now, that's not so bad for a skinny Jewish kid."

If praying is a productive way for a floor trader to acquire an edge, the man who ought to know about it is Kenneth Khouri. He is a curly-haired young trader with a corner-mouth grin whom I run into near the Mesa post one afternoon as he is moving, somewhat stealthily, toward the cafeteria. Khouri is a born-again Christian, and proud of it. A button prominently pinned to his smock declares "Praise the Lord." Though traders invariably consider it critical to be on the floor at the opening bell, Khouri shuffles on at ten-thirty. The reasons are manifold: he doesn't like to wake up too early, it takes him an hour to drive in from his home in New Jersey, and he refuses to budge until he's put in an hour's worth of solid praying. Khouri came to options via a circuitous route. He worked as a clerk for an over-the-counter trading firm; served as an over-the-counter trader himself, until his firm was smothered by debt; worked as a retail broker in Florida; became a distributor of smoke alarms in New York. That, apparently, is when God intervened. "At this point, I prayed for God to bless the business or get me out of it," Khouri tells me. "After what I would consider divine guidance, I felt led to go into the stock business. In May of 1978 I was able to buy the lowest-priced options seat that had been offered. I paid ten thousand dollars. It's been, quite frankly, the toughest business I've ever been in, the reason being that you have to have a lot of internal fortitude to muster up and overcome your fears, your timidity. In the rest of society we're basically submitting ourselves to our emotions, but down here you have to really weed out your emotions. When you're in a crowd and short and a stock is moving up and everybody and his mother is buying the stock, you have to stand there cold-bloodedly and not panic. That was the most difficult thing I had to learn down here—that cold-blooded feeling."

Apparently Khouri got the hang of it, because he informs me proudly that he ran off a skein of twenty-eight consecutive profitable months before he dropped a couple of thousand dollars in March 1981. "I have the Lord to thank for that," he hastens to add.

"How do you trade?"

"I try to void myself of the public mentality, which is 'I think the market is a buy and therefore I shall buy it.' I try to read what the market is telling me. I can't affect the market:

I can only make a short-term dent. So the market is going to do whatever it's going to do. Instinct and feel have nothing to do with it. You have to read what the market is saying. I read supply and demand. I use charts as a tool. It's almost like a pro quarterback. When he looks over the defense, he reads what it's going to do."

"Does God ever pitch in, pick a promising option or two?" I mumble, a little uneasy about trespassing on delicate arrangements.

"Only once," he says. "It was October of 1978 or 1979, one of the October massacres when the market fell apart. I was walking across the floor from Tandy to go to the Bally options because I thought the market was going to rally. I can show you the spot on the floor where it happened. [He does, though to my nondenominational eye the segment looks like any other part of the floor, maybe a little dirtier.] I walked into a vale, for lack of a better word. My eyes just opened and I could see that the market was going to fall appreciably in the short term."

"So what did you do?"

"Oh, I got short. And I had a profitable month when lots of others were losing their shirts. But I can't take credit. I have to give it to God."

Harry's at the American Exchange, nestled below the trading floor, is a welcoming sort of place. Since it is the favored breakfast nook of many of the Amex traders and brokers, it is necessary to get there before eight o'clock or you'll have trouble being seated no matter how fat your bank roll is. At about a quarter to ten, though, the place, almost as if by decree, begins to empty systematically. You can tell when the opening of trading is at hand, not by consulting your

Rolex watch, but by sensing the quiet that envelops Harry's. A quick glance around the room, where the bulk of tables are filled with besmocked individuals, would almost make one think he had come upon an artists' colony. The Harry of Harry's is Harry Poulakakos, a genial, silver-haired Greek who told me over a drink once that he's happiest when the markets are roaring and his traders are raking it in. As for his own market plunges, he would rather not discuss them in even the sketchiest terms.

In a table against the far wall, Katz is downing a breakfast of two eggs up, sausage, and grapefruit juice, while explaining to me how he came to a career of puts and calls. He was reared in the pleasant suburb of Englewood, New Jersey. His father was a civil engineer, but eventually dropped that career to take over his own father's clothing store. Katz's father possessed a considerable aptitude for math. Katz read his books and also received informal instruction from his father as he was growing up. "I always enjoyed playing with numbers," he says. Katz eventually got a Ph.D. in statistics at the University of Pennsylvania, and while moving toward it, he worked for Penn Central, doing economic research in their marketing department. "After I got my degree, I found a job with the New York Stock Exchange in its research department. They were looking for someone with regulatory experience—there were still fixed brokerage commission rates then, but the issue of unfixing them was under exploration, and so they needed someone who could testify and write testimony for regulatory bodies. Two or three years later, the stock exchange looked at the possibility of options. I always dabbled a little in options on my own, and since few New York Stock Exchange people knew much about options, almost by default I got on the options committee. I did a lot of technical work there. Two years into the project, the

American Stock Exchange decided to expand their program (they already had a limited number of options) and offered something like a hundred and thirty-eight seats at fifteen thousand dollars a seat. At the same time that this occurred, the options project at the New York Stock Exchange was hitting all sorts of snags, and it didn't look like they would get into options. At that point—I never liked working for anyone else anyway, and with the frustration of the project—I said, 'Ah, the hell with it, I'll try it for a year.' I took all of my capital and borrowed a small amount from my parents: I needed the fifteen thousand for the seat, and there was a minimum capital requirement of twenty-five thousand dollars. My wife and I had just bought a house, and so we weren't exactly rolling in dough. I knew nothing about trading, but I used to find excuses to go down to the floor when I was at the New York Exchange. You go down there and you pick up the language. You pick up an ear for the floor. It's very hard to hear things down there if you're not trained to listen."

I break into Katz's narrative to ask him to clarify why, given that he lacked any trading experience, he had the hubris to think he could make a career at such a risky calling.

"I had a high opinion of myself," he says, without pause. "I was nervous, all right, but I felt that there was room for a highly mathematical approach to the trading of options. I basically learned by trial and error. The first day was scary. I was scared. The one good piece of advice I got was that you have to crawl before you walk. I was trading in ones and fives, and it's a good thing, because I lost money the first month. In fact, I got creamed the first month. But I figured you have to pay for an education. If you want to get a medical degree or a law degree, then you have to pay the tuition, and you don't get any money back from that. And that's what I was doing: I was paying tuition. It's the same way I learned pinochle."

Katz pauses to wolf down some eggs and sip some juice, then picks up the story. "I lost money for a couple of months. I made a small amount the third month. After the first six months, I was only down a small amount. The big hit came in April. Up until then, I was marginally ahead. I was following the conventional wisdom of the floor. That April was the now famous Big April. The market jumped about a hundred points in two days, mainly because of heavy foreign investing. It caught just about everybody on the floor short. I didn't know how to cover risk possibilities that well. The upshot was that I lost about twenty thousand dollars in the two days. I was really close to the edge. I got fairly discouraged, to say the least, and I did three things. I rewrote my résumé and decided I would at least start looking for other job possibilities. I started talking to people around the floor to see if there was anyone who wanted to put up some capital to back me. And, third, I put everything I had done wrong in April, on a day-to-day basis, into the computer and let the computer run for hours and hours. Basically, I asked the computer what would have saved me—what should I have done?"

The computer, being the fastest to respond, told Katz that the conventional philosophy of traders, which was primarily to sell call options and buy stock as a hedge, was wrong. "The computer said that all sorts of other possibilities were better—options spread against options, shorting stock and going long options, reverse conversions. People used to do the same thing day in and day out, regardless of the circumstances. I became more flexible. It's sort of like a manager who always thinks of bunting. Well, once the batter's got two strikes on him he better stop thinking about bunting, unless the guy's a pretty damned good bunter. He better let the guy swing away. So far as the other things I did, I talked to other people on the floor. A lot of them had gotten hurt, and so they were sort of lukewarm to deals of any kind. Some people were totally wiped out by those two days. To get a deal, I basically would have to give away more than I got. I put out my résumé and went to a couple of interviews for jobs involving economic research of different sorts. Every time I went for an interview, I realized how much I hated working for someone else. It made me realize why I had quit in the first place. Incidentally, an important aspect during this time was my wife, who was fantastic. She put no pressure on me to do something more stable. Well, to wrap things up, I made in May what I had lost in April, and June was a very profitable month for me. So my year at trading was up and I was convinced that my change in trading strategy had put me onto something. I've never had any doubts about my profession since."

Among the rewards trading has brought Katz is a net worth safely into seven figures, though he subscribes to more of a five-figure life-style. He lives in an unassuming two-story colonial home in Princeton Junction, New Jersey. His wife is an artist and works from the house. Typically, Katz boards a seven o'clock train to Newark, where he switches to a PATH train that deposits him beneath the World Trade Center. After a brisk stroll, he usually reaches the Amex locker room by a bit after eight. To get to the train, he drives a 1974 Vega that's rusting and leaks whenever it rains. ("What am I going to do with a new car at a train-station parking lot?") Tennis and skiing are his main forms of recreation. "I'm not a flashy person," Katz will say. "I'm not into material things. The only things I indulge myself in are travel and electronic toys. I have the computer and a videotape recorder. A nice hi-fi. I intend to be one of the first ones to buy a flat-screen TV. I suppose at some point I'll buy a satellite dish."

"The money hasn't changed you at all?" I asked Katz once.

He pondered that a moment, then replied, "Instead of changing the spark plugs on the lawn mower, I hired a gardener last year. That's the major change in my life-style."

Mesa down. Tandy up. Mesa further down. Mesa up. The swings in the options are hypnotizing. Also frustrating. When is a downward move a plunge down a mineshaft? When has an upward climb peaked? When to sell and when to keep running?

When I ask Katz during a particularly discombobulating period whether he believes in signs or patterns or market voodoo, he replies crisply, "I'm a natural skeptic. I don't believe in long-term anything. If something goes down, I believe it will eventually go up. A lot of people believe in trends. I believe in reversals of trends. It's just my nature to be skeptical. When anything happens, there's a bandwagon effect. It puts a floor on a decline and a roof on a rise. I never care that much about one individual trade. If somebody offers me two-to-one on the flip of a coin and I choose heads and it comes up tails, I don't say I made a bad bet. I say, Let me do it two or three more times and I'll come out ahead."

"What if you flip the coin ten times and lose every time?"

"Then I have to start looking at the coin."

He rubs his fist against his forehead and goes on: "I'm skeptical about analysis of any sort. I think the thing that bothers me most is hindsight. Everyone has twenty-twenty hindsight. Sports is the epitome of this. A team loses three games in a row and they're in a slump. Baloney! The New York Islanders lose three games and everybody and his sister writes about this terrible slump. It's a good team. The losses mean nothing. I mean, three losses in a row is a trend? Everybody has an answer. This is what really bothers me. People like to have an answer. They don't want to believe that things happen randomly."

"Are you skeptical about everything—the weather, relationships, garage mechanics, food prices?" I ask.

"Except for politics," Katz replies. "I am a firm believer in the conspiracy theory of politics. I was the first one of my friends who believed that Lee Harvey Oswald was part of a broad conspiracy and that the government knew about it and let it happen to avoid a war with Russia or something. I think when they open up the archives it will be shown that Johnson and Warren knew about it. I believe all of politics is like that."

The morning slides by and lunchtime arrives. No food, however, enters Katz's stomach. Don't you eat lunch? I ask. "I prefer two meals a day," Katz says. "Before I worked here, I would eat lunch and dinner. Now I eat breakfast and dinner. If I ate three meals a day, my weight would just balloon. Many people down here don't eat. I take juice during the day to keep up my energy. Juice is the key. Without juice, who knows what would happen."

Activity slows enough during the lunch hour that Bobby Van Caneghan, the put specialist, takes out a hand exerciser. "I'm going for my record," he announces to no one in particular. He counts off to fifteen. His hand surrenders.

Mopping his brow, Van Caneghan strolls away from his post and says to Katz, "You stare at that screen long enough and your eyes start to go."

"So does your mind," Katz says. "Look at this guy here," and he points to a man who appears to have recently crossed into his forties. "He's only twelve years old, and just look at him."

Katz tugs at my sleeve and directs my attention to a sheet of paper Scotch-taped to my back. I am, according to the sign, up for sale.

A slack period is the absolute worst time to visit the floor of the Amex or, for that matter, any trading floor. Unless you do a good job of remaining unobtrusive, you end up the butt of a good many pranks and hoary jokes. One of the advantages of being an independent trader is the freedom to remain infantile well beyond your time, and thus a sense of humor is an ironclad prerequisite to survival on the floor. Having personally been indoctrinated into the shenanigans, I can attest to many of the favorite stunts. The most popular trick is to affix signs or various paper weaponry to someone's back, disguising the deed by clapping the victim firmly and telling him what a great chap he is. Arrows quivering from bull's-eyes and hatchets are the most common weapons I spotted stuck on people's backs. Signs run the gamut of conventional nonsense: "Post No Bills," "Burt Reynolds Look Alike," "Wimp of the Month," "Kill This Man." Stanley Katz once had someone tape "Suits Altered for Free" to his jacket. I noticed several individuals unwittingly bearing makeshift Red Cross flags. I have had '74 Cutlasses and '76 Pontiacs advertised for sale on my back. I have also been outfitted with a sign reading "Ask Him How's the Job," and politely and bewilderingly went about informing a half-dozen strangers that my job was quite satisfying before I sensed what was up.

Another frivolous prank is to sneak up on someone and affix paper spurs to the back of his shoes. One becomes aware he has been thus victimized when he starts to hear increasing numbers of Indian war whoops from passing traders. If someone races by and hoots, "It's snowing in New York," then you know you've fallen prey to the other common shoe stunt, which involves slyly coating a trader's footwear with talcum powder while he is preoccupied with conversation. After my formerly black shoes had turned snow-white one day, I was told, as commiseration, that there was no reason to feel bad. After all, several governors of states had gotten the same treatment. "This is why no one would sell his seat at any price," Katz told me after one especially active spell of pranks. "You don't have to grow up."

Traders often wonder what will happen to them once they move into their late forties or fifties. When they look around, they see they are surrounded by guys in their twenties and thirties. There is such a thing as the fifty- or sixty-year-old trader, but he's a rarity. Usually he's got plenty of money salted away, and he trades, for limited hours, because he can't give up the high. But it's tough. One trader, still safely in his twenties, joked to me, "At forty, a trader can't hold a cup and saucer without their constantly rattling. His hair is either entirely gray or entirely gone. The strongest thing he drinks is Bosco, his ulcer's so bad. He's in worse shape than a pro football player at forty. He'd probably feel pretty damned grim, if it weren't for the fact that the guy's worth a million or so." Gray hair is not uncommon on the Amex floor, though most of it grows prematurely on the heads of men still in their twenties and thirties. I met one trader who owned up to being fifty-one, and he speculated, presumably from rumblings in his stomach, that he was one of the five elders of the floor. The thought of it made him pale a bit, and he quickly elected to take his mind off the topic by making a few trades.

"I would think options, by their very nature, are geared

more to the young person," Katz tells me when I ask him about age and options. "There's the incredible strain. There's the tremendous amount of concentration. The roller-coaster pattern options can take is wearying. I would think you could quickly burn yourself out. I can't imagine myself doing this past another ten years. I think you have to eventually lose the concentration. It's like a goaltender in hockey. Sure, there's a guy like Glenn Hall, who played into his forties and kept kicking the pucks out. But that's rare. Concentration, quick thinking, reflexes are all very important in options. You can't do it beyond a certain age. Some do, and you really have to admire them."

What does Katz expect to be doing ten years from now?

"I'll probably still continue to keep a finger in trading. I might try to find a young kid and lease my seat to him and teach him my techniques, sort of pass the baton along. Who knows? I might go into teaching, or I might write a book."

Early in 1981, it became clear to me (as it becomes painfully clear to any trader early in his learning curve) how quickly the hills of money can wash away. In the space of a single week in mid-March, three mammoth merger proposals swept across the financial markets like one tidal wave crashing on top of another. Standard Oil of California bid some four billion dollars for AMAX, in what was then the meatiest merger offer in corporate history. Then Seagram & Sons dangled a bit more than two billion dollars in front of St. Joe Minerals and, before Wall Street could catch its breath, Sohio and Kennecott entered into a merger agreement valued at close to 1.8 billion dollars. Apparently a number of investors got at least a vague inkling of all these deals before they were publicly announced—exactly how was not determined, but there are countless ways in which so-called inside information seeps out of corporate chambers. Also, a number of investors presumably got extremely lucky.

In any event, there were floods of orders for the options of all three takeover targets in the days and hours immediately preceding the announcement of the merger bids. The March options, due to expire in only a week, were trading well out of the money; in other words, their strike prices were substantially higher than those at which the underlying stocks were trading. June options were equally unappetizing. Few, if any, professional options traders would have been long in those particular months; it would be much like placing a bet on the seventy-to-one shot as the horses entered the stretch with the seventy-to-one horse limping along twenty lengths off the pace dragging his jockey in the dirt. The computers of traders and their own common sense tell them to sell overpriced options short. Thus, when the raft of orders arrived, a good many market specialists and traders went naked short. It seemed like taking money from a baby. The improbable, of course, happened. The merger bids came. The per-share prices were well beyond what the takeover stocks were trading at. Up rocketed prices. The seemingly worthless options turned gold. The options traders who had sold the contracts short were compelled either to buy shares of the stock or else to buy back options at a much higher price than they had been selling at just a few days earlier; either way, the losses would be awesome. Some traders dropped more than a million dollars. Some options firms took drubbings on the order of ten or twenty million. The Chicago Board Options Exchange suspended seven members from trading, since their liquid capital dipped below the minimum from losses suffered in Kennecott options. Kennecott shares, after the merger news, soared more than twenty-six dollars in a single day. It understandably grated on many traders to learn that the son of an AMAX director, just prior to the AMAX bid, had snapped up six hundred options to buy AMAX shares at fifty bucks a share. The options cost roughly $3,750. Two days after the California Standard offer, they were said to be worth a cool million dollars.

"It was an improbable and unfortunate thing, and it's one of the loaded mines that we can walk on any day down here," I was told by one options trader who had luckily not been burned by the events. "We work with computers, and the chance of something like this happening was infinitesimal. The public probably made a lot of money, but there was a lot of blood on this floor. We trade value and the public trades emotion. This time, the emotionalists won."

Ever since I heard about those calamitous events, I have been eager to talk to a trader who dropped a bundle of money—not fifty thousand or a hundred thousand dollars, the sort of pocket change that all traders blow every now and then, but a truly breathtaking sum. One day months later I am lolling near the Mesa post when I drift into a casual conversation with a trader and I happen to remark that a lot of professionals are quick to talk about their killings but clam up when it comes to their ravagings. He looks me squarely in the face and, without even a tremor of anxiety, says right away, "Well, I lost a million dollars in one day. I don't mind telling you that."

The man is William Toll. He is rugged-looking (he reminds me of Chuck Connors or someone who belongs before a campfire in a Camel ad), thirty-six, with an antic look about him. "Yeah, it was a bad day," he goes on. "It may have been the worst day ever had by someone on this floor." The massive loss came in Kennecott options, and when I asked whether it was actually a million dollars, Toll did some quick figuring and cheerfully corrected the figure to a million and fifty thousand.

"That's trading," he says, shrugging, when I press him on how he took the debacle. "It was over and done with."

After he peeled off the bills to pay the debt, Toll tells me, he was still left with a tidy inventory, in round figures, of maybe eight hundred thousand dollars, so he was able to eat a proper dinner that night, which presumably helped him keep his wits about him. But he says that he didn't even need a stiff drink to get over the vanished million. "Nah, I don't like to drink."

"Did you do anything different that night?" I ask, incredulous at his insouciance.

"I might have gone to bed early," he says.

Toll travels in the fast lane, playing one of the very riskiest games on the options floor. He has no interest in aping the strategies of the bulk of the Amex traders, which tend to be too gingerly for his tastes. He just likes to roll the bones; what comes, comes. His specific method is to sell deep out-of-the-money call options, options whose strike price is higher than the stock price and which are thus likely to expire worthless. He trades them big, risking money as if it were birdseed, and he trades them naked, without protecting himself by buying stock positions, taking the chance that they won't be exercised. The individual profits on out-of-the-money options are measly, and so you've got to be right an overwhelming majority of times to cash in big. The catch is that the few times you may be wrong—when the stock makes a dramatic move against your position and finds you short—the losses can buckle your knees. Toll is something like the downhill ski racer who thinks nothing of going out when the slopes are sheer ice and visibility is about three inches. "The technique," Toll explains to me, "is called 'bang 'em and pray.'"

Toll is able to treat his hard times with a belligerent humor and a measure of philosophizing. "I get depressed when I'm wrong," he says, "but I've been down here five years and I've been wrong maybe five times. I came down into this business with under a hundred thousand dollars and I'm worth a couple of million now, so the business has been good to me. This business is risk-reward. I take big risks and I get big rewards. Every so often my number comes up and I take a bath. Most times, though, the wheel stops somewhere else."

Before gravitating to the floor, Toll entertained a number of identities. He acquired an MBA at Columbia; served in the Army for three years, including a stint in Vietnam ("You want to talk about risks, talk about Vietnam"); worked as a financial analyst at Mobil Oil ("I liked that job") and then at W. R. Grace ("A monkey could do that job"); worked as a retail broker for Merrill Lynch; then came down to the floor in March 1977, finding the hullabaloo almost instantly paradisal ("I always wanted to do things on my own. I never liked taking orders").

"Few people are like myself, who just sell," Toll says to me. "I'm instinctive. I trade off psychology. I know when something strange happens. You can hear that things are different. To know this game, you have to be a student of mass psychology. I can smell when someone thinks he knows something."

After the Kennecott savaging, friends of Toll who had been frowning on his nerve-racking ways told him that maybe now he would come to his senses and change his style before his pockets were altogether empty. Giving away a million bucks, they sneered, you're a fool. Play the game the way it should be played. But Toll was convinced in his bones that his principles were correct. With majestic disdain, he started trading naked options even bigger. "I made a million and a quarter in the remaining nine months of the year," he says with a resilient laugh.

"Why do you like the big risks?" I ask.

"Maybe there's something like if you live on the razor's edge you feel more alive," he says after a moment or two. "I don't really believe any of that, but I know I like risks. It's also like getting into a hot tub. If you just jump in, you scream from the pain. If you get in with a toe and then ease in, it's okay. That's the way it's been with me down here. I would take five hundred options and say, Wow! Then sixteen thousand. Wow! You get used to the risks. That's why the Kennecott thing was like falling off a log. I had been taking big risks so long."

For all his accumulated wealth, Toll, like Katz, is a virtual nonspender. About his only material asset is a car—a Le Car, a vehicle he can barely squeeze into. He rents an apartment on 113th Street. He is single.

When I wonder what he is piling up the money for, Toll just strokes his jaw and squints. "I guess I'm in here for the sport."

Insider trading, which is illegal though offenders rarely get punished, is a sexy topic that gets bandied about around the floors and locker rooms of exchanges, and so I broached the subject to Katz one morning and asked him for his observations.

"There are two types of inside information, as far as I can see," he replied. "There is the type that the public is familiar with, which gets written up in the newspapers, which there are scandals over. Advance knowledge of a merger, advance

knowledge of a big oil find—that kind of thing. It's very difficult to deal with, and it's annoying, all right. You can get
burned pretty bad by it. There are certain brokerage firms
that have the ability—by virtue of their clients—to get a
good bit of inside information, and you learn to beware of
them. Let's face it, suppose you're a broker for Merrill
Lynch, just to randomly pick a name, and you have accounts
of four officers of one company and, lo and behold, one day
all four call you up and say they want to buy strong in Yakke
Company. What would you deduce? I sure as hell would
deduce that something was in the works. So the broker may
call up a few of his heavy-hitting accounts and say, Look, I
don't know what's going on for sure, but I have a hunch, and
why don't you try some Yakke stock or some Yakke options.
There may be really hot action as a result, and some traders
take a bath. There's not much you can do about something
like that as a trader. About the only thing you can do is call a
company and point out that there's all this activity and all
these rumors, and try to find out if anything's going on. I did
that once. About a year ago, there was a hard-driving interest in Mesa that started from two brokerage houses that will
remain nameless. I decided to call the secretary of a guy I
knew at Mesa. It was very odd. She acted as if she were
reading from a piece of paper. She told me that she had been
instructed not to put calls through until the company had
made an announcement. It was clear as day that the company was going to make a major announcement. I mean, the
woman was practically reading like a machine. At that point,
I pulled in my horns and I didn't go short. I bought every
put I could and every call I could, figuring the stock was
going to move a lot. It did. The announcement came the next
day, and it concerned a significant joint venture with Texaco.

"The second type of inside information is different. The

technical name is 'front-running' or 'tape-racing.' What happens is, somebody knows a large block of stock is for sale, and so they sell options every which way they can, and we buy them. Suddenly a ten-thousand-share block comes across the tape, down a point, and we're stuck. That's much more annoying than the other kind of inside information. Two or three years ago, tape-racing was very common. There were institutional firms that had reputations for practicing it. Some rules have since been rewritten and enforcement has gotten a bit better, so it's not quite as common or blatant. But it still happens—I'd say, about once every month in a given stock—and it's damn hard to prove. I've been burned enough by it to remember who did it to me. When I first started out, I used to complain to the exchange and to the firm in question. They didn't do anything about it. They all had excuses. But it costs me a couple of thousand bucks at a time, and so I let the broker who brought the order know I'm mad and make sure the firm gets the message in no uncertain terms."

All in all, Katz views inside information and its reverberations as inevitable risks of his craft, like excavated teeth in ice hockey or failed brakes in auto racing. "Somebody's always going to know something in advance," he says. "The secrets always get out. The people who get burned are annoyed. The people who don't get burned are happy. And the people who make a real killing keep a low profile."

"Did you ever get any inside information of any value?" I ask.

"You get tips and rumors all the time," he says. "Literally all the time. I'd say that fifty percent of what you hear doesn't come to pass. You get days when they're buying Mesa all over the place and the rumor goes around that Mesa had a big find in western Arizona or something like that. And you wait and wait and it never happens. You just don't know what credence to give to these things. If the rumor comes from a big enough house, you have to figure that a lot of people know it and act accordingly. If the rumor, say, comes from a Merrill Lynch broker, well, Merrill Lynch has an awful lot of brokers and controls a lot down here. So whether the rumor is true or false, it's going to affect things, and so you act on it."

A crowded Harry's. Ten to fifteen minutes to get seated, enough time to blow a fortune upstairs. Katz and I have spilled into a booth with one of his closest friends on the floor. Eggs and sausage for Katz. Just coffee for the friend, whose name is Hyman Muller. Much of his hair is gone, though much of the vacancy is covered by a yarmulke. Muller thereby boasts one of the most recognizable heads on the Amex floor. He is a somewhat overweight man with a moon face and a flinty look in his eyes. During trading sessions, he often breaks into a state of barely controlled frenzy, as if a bucket of ice had just been dropped down his back. Like Katz, Muller bows to a computer. He is also a volatility spreader.

"Options is the only game where you can quantify your risk," Muller is saying by way of explaining why he gravitated to options. "You can't do it in stocks and you can't do it in commodities. You can't define your risks to a penny. I can't quantify my risk in anything else—whether it's real estate, art, or garbage pails."

"But the money's biggest in commodities, isn't it?" I say.

"Yeah, you can make the most money, because of the leverage," Muller says. "You can have no money and make a fortune. By the same token, you can have a fortune and get blown out the next day."

A trader slips into a seat at the table next to us and, over-hearing the tail end of the conversation, says, "Hey, Hyman, I didn't know you knew what a commodity was."

Muller says, "I know what commodities are. I had money in this pocket and now I don't."

"But you have a pocket."

"I'm not sure."

"You know, you should leave those eggs on the table and sell December eggs against them," Katz chimes in.

"Take those eggs home in a paper bag and go short," Muller says.

We get around to the subject of how far options traders might go in exposing themselves to risk.

"A lot of people down here would not write naked calls or puts, and I'm one of them," Muller says. "The odds may be eighty percent that you're right. But I don't want to live with the other twenty percent. That's blood money. I don't want it. My main position is to be able to sleep at night. I have a very low threshold for pain and for staying awake at night."

"He's the Sominex trader," the man at the next table comments.

"It's the Muller Insomnia Rule," Muller says. "If you can't sleep with your position, don't put it on."

"When did you learn that?" I ask.

"The first November I was down here. I was short a hundred out-of-the-money calls and got murdered. It made quite a big impression on me and on my wallet."

Later, as Katz moves onto the trading floor, he remarks, "Basically, the ones who don't make it in this business don't have patience. They need action. They have to be in on every trade. They have to turn on a dime. They are constantly writhing. They have to show that they're big guys and can trade a thousand contracts. They can be goaded into making a bad trade by someone who tries to goad them into it. They can get burned. Everyone here tries to psych everyone else. I have it done to me. I do it. It's part of the game."

Katz likes to recite certain psychological ploys that come into play on the floor and can bear on one's fortune—I have seen wily maneuvers work on an unsuspecting trader like catnip on a cat. On psychological warfare, Katz says: "There's a lot of psychology in terms of the size people bid and offer. People are always trying to convince someone that something is a good deal. One way they do it is they'll scream an offer very loudly, hoping that somebody will quickly take it and not realize that it's a bad sale. The level of the voice can convey a certain importance to an offer. You find out that some people are more subject to emotional mistakes than others. There are a lot of people who try psychology and a lot of people who succumb to it. That's why you need discipline."

"Do you use psychological warfare?" I ask.

"If the right people are in the crowd, sure. I'll do it. There are traders I know I can manipulate into giving me a few things. There are ways of making a market to get things. Most good traders you can't do it with. You take advantage when you can. And you're not necessarily taking advantage. Someone may have bought something at seven and they're happy to get rid of it at seven and an eighth. You don't always know when you're taking advantage of someone. They may be taking advantage of you."

"Can an individual like you move the price of an option?" I ask.

"Oh, sure. It's like anything else. It's like a poker game. You would be in effect pulling off a bluff."

"How much can you move it?"

"Not that much. You're moving it only to the point where people decide it's warranted or it's not warranted. You can't move prices on a sustained basis. Not for more than a couple of days. That's very risky."

Hearing about such things prompts me to ask Katz if he is bothered by any barbs of conscience that he is feasting off the gullibility of the public. "Traders make money off the naïveté of the public," he says. "But that's the way it is in most businesses. Let's face it, if everyone knew how to repair his car, garage mechanics could not charge the fees they charge. I could build a house myself, but I wouldn't want to live in any house I built. Most of the profits come about because you have expertise and you are making money off offering it. The novice doesn't have the expertise, and what he needs is the liquidity to get a reasonable price. You're giving the trader profit to get liquidity."

"Why do you trade?" I ask Katz.

"Everything I do is me," he shoots back. "If I have a bad day, I only have myself to blame. If I have a good day, I only have myself to credit. I have a high opinion of myself. When I worked for others, I always felt I was doing better than I was being paid or getting credit for. That's very annoying for someone with a big ego. There's also a satisfaction that I'm playing a mathematical game, and it's interesting to me that all the math I got in school is paying off this way. I'll bet my math teachers never quite intended this sort of application. And, I should add, this is fun. It's a hell of a lot of fun doing this."

Trading is basically gambling, though, isn't it? I say.

"I look on this as gambling in the sense that Harrah's looks on a casino as gambling," is Katz's reply. "I'm the house. I don't like playing against the odds. I only like being the house."

When he is away from the puts and calls of the American Stock Exchange, Katz is fond of playing cards for modest stakes. He went through college locked in a card game virtually every free moment. He is quick to venture out to the horse races when he can find the time. "I love to watch the horses run," he will say. "I love race tracks. I've been going to them since I was ten years old. I love picking winners. But no matter how much I like to go to the horses, I'm only a two-dollar bettor."

"Yoooooooooo!" a floor broker screeches. It seems to be a popular call. So is "Heeey!" expressed at sonic-boom level. "Yooooo" again. A few "Heeey"s.

A cool, breezy morning. Katz, as usual, is at the Mesa post early, bantering affably with the specialists. Someone has clipped out an ad of Jim Palmer seductively flaunting his Jockey briefs, not to mention his own imposing physique, and taped it to the counter. Underneath has been appended the words "Lease a man by the hour or the week." Katz is saying that his wife is throwing a party for a local art group and he has been appointed to pick up the tab for the food— seventy dollars. A pinchpenny amount, considering the sums he risks each day, but he feels the outlay makes it necessary to do particularly well today. Yesterday, he got himself into a hole, having bought a good deal of Mesa stock in a declining market that seems likely to keep declining. He has decided to sell two thousand shares at whatever the opening price is, before the stock tumbles further. "I'm going to take my losses and get on with things," he explains.

Besides his trading earnings, Katz has a curious investment that pays handsome dividends. The investment is an
old college buddy who, until a couple of years ago, was
a practicing psychologist in Philadelphia. He groused at
length to Katz that he wanted to make "real" money, as opposed to the mere stratospheric income a psychologist pulls
down ("He's got big eyes," Katz told me). All right, Katz said
to him, I'll buy you a seat on the Philadelphia Stock Exchange and stake you with some capital, and I get a split of
your profits, presuming there are some. The man had never
visited a trading floor in his life. In effect, Katz groomed him
by long-distance phone. At first, he would trek to Katz's
home on weekends to do runs on Katz's computer. Now he
has his own machine. Katz would have been thrilled if his
rookie friend had broken even his first six months. Instead,
the friend chalked up one of the hottest debuts ever seen on
the Philly floor. Asked to explain this, Katz responds, "He
had the best teacher."

Once Mesa opens, the activity is unusually furious. Traders are unloading options at every price movement. The
stock has plummeted three and a half points in the last two
days. People are bailing out.

"I am a known pervert," a sunny-faced broker in a green
smock declares as he stomps into the cluster of traders.

"Not only is he a known pervert," Katz says, "but he is a
renowned pervert. If you wanted a pervert, you couldn't find
a better one than him."

The broker peers pensively at the Mesa put screen. He
whistles in mock disbelief. "Ah, a quality issue," he drawls.
"It goes down a half a point a day."

"One a day," Katz quickly corrects him. "One a day. It's a
multiple vitamin."

Dean Bruskof, a short, stocky trader I had met who commutes from Philadelphia, wanders by. He taps me on the arm and says, almost boastfully, "Look here, I just made a very bad decision. I got my ass handed to me."

"What happened?" I ask.

"I bought fifty calls of Standard Oil of California. I felt the oils were due for a little bit of a rally. I'm getting my head crushed."

"What are you going to do?"

He wrinkles his nose. "It's hard to discern. I'll stick with it. I'm bagged right now."

He chuckles and vanishes into the depths of the floor, like a sheik looking for the next oasis.

Another trader in the crowd, hair tumbling over his temples, falls into conversation with me about trading ability. "You can't put a finger on what makes a great trader," he says. "There's a guy down here who's one of the biggest and most successful traders. I've known him since we were kids. I always did much better than him in school. I went to college and law school. He didn't finish college. He makes a multiple of what I make, and I'm no slouch."

He has huge sliding eyes, and he uses them to make a sour inspection of the tubes, then goes on: "Some of the best bridge players and backgammon players are options traders. It's an arbitrage mentality—offsetting risks."

He tells me that his own favorite play is something he identifies as the "strangle." He elaborates: "Say the stock is at twenty-two. The twenty-five calls are out of the money. The twenty-five puts are out. You sell them both. It's sort of a hybrid straddle."

I nod vaguely, but he has already leapt to other thoughts. "I've seen a lot of flops. If you've been here four or five years, *ipso facto* you've proved that you can do it. Everything good or bad that can happen to you has happened to you several times by then."

He smiles, and his chest seems to expand like a balloon filling up with air. "You have to have a big ego to trade well," he says. "You have to stick your neck out. To buy something when it's going down, believe me, you have to have a big ego."

Voices ring in staccato spurts.

"Hey, Bobby, how are the twenties?"

"Got a hundred to go."

"Hey, Curly, April fifteens, what's the bid?"

"Bobby, I'll do that twice."

"You letting your hair grow, Bobby? Looks nice."

"You wearing a hair net, Bobby? Looks good."

"Sell six at a quarter to Drexel Burnham."

"Look at that Cooper Industries. Finally back to where they crucified me."

"Exalted leader, how are they?"

A chubby, bearded broker shambles over and hands some orders to the specialist.

"Garbage, garbage," the broker grumbles. "I feel like the garbage man."

"You are the garbage man," Katz says.

"Listen, without this garbage, guys like you wouldn't be eating."

Katz says, "Without guys like us, you wouldn't have anyone to play with."

"I don't need you to play with. I play with myself."

"Then you really are the garbage man."

The hours whirl by. The Mesa trend doesn't improve much; it's hard sledding for Katz just to stay even. When the closing bell finally sounds, he seems relieved. He tidies up his sheets. The day was just okay, he says. Will he push harder tomorrow, take bigger positions?

"No," he says. "That's how some guys do it. Not me. I try to keep my discipline. I'm a big believer in the saying that you can't dance every dance."

THREE

inter has come to Chicago, and with it the city's numbing winds. Down at the head of busy LaSalle Street, the wind whips against the squat Board of Trade building. Even the six-ton statue of Ceres, Roman goddess of agriculture, that perches atop the roof, looks chilly. Morning commuters are tangling on the streets. Horns honk. Tires squeal. Oblivious of the frigid temperature, Steve Stone, with only a thin windbreaker to shield him from the weather, couldn't care less how cold it is. Striding through the wind, hands dug into his pants pockets, he is preoccupied only with the fact that he's running late. "We've got thirty minutes till the beans open," he says. "Gotta be there for the bean opening. Who knows what those beans are going to do today."

Just trying to get onto the floor can be an anxiety-ridden experience. During the early morning hours, the elevators rising to the fourth-floor trading room are jammed to a point just short of asphyxiation. They are a prelude to the maddening pace and congestion of the Board of Trade. When the doors slide open on four, Stone spills (or, more accurately, is spilled) into the hallway, where he courses past the early arrivals who slump splay-legged in cushioned chairs along the wall, puffing on cigarettes and running their eyes over the odds on this Sunday's pro football matchups. This is a gambler's heaven, where if you so desire you can probably pick up decent action on what color shoes somebody is going to show up in. At the newsstand in the lobby there are no fewer than six football tip sheets (such as *The Huddle, Winning Points, Score*). Some of the traders deposit their street shoes on carpeted racks against the wall and then slip into soft-soles. Stone's feet are already encased in Hush Puppies, so he trundles sleepily over to the marble-sheathed coat-check room, turns in his windbreaker, and shrugs into a cherry-colored smock. Smoothing out the wrinkles, he light-foots it onto the trading floor.

Steve Stone (not his real name: he was more bashful than most traders I ran across) is a soybean futures trader, or a "local," as the floor traders here are called. His workday consists of four hours of standing in a huge wooden pit screaming his lungs out. He gets pounded and kicked, pencils are jabbed in his face, his toes are squashed, and he is often hoarse and bone-tired by the end of the day. It's easy to become a bit unstuck. "I'll tell you, I never need a sleeping pill at night; I'm half-dead," he says. "I often need a drink, though." When he first appeared on the Board of Trade floor four years ago, he tried his voice at corn. After three days of yelling in the corn pit, he defected to the bean pit, then the home of the most fickle commodity on the exchange, and he quickly became infatuated and has been there ever since. "I really like the beans. They don't fool around. They really move." Like many commodity traders, Stone is young. He is twenty-seven, boyish-looking, chunky, with a rock-ribbed face and tousled brown hair. He has a bouncy walk that suggests someone who is in tiptop physical shape, and a baritone voice that gives him the sort of booming, body-shattering projection that does for commodity traders what twenty-twenty vision does for a race-car driver. Beneath his cherry smock, courtesy of Gulf, Great-Lakes Grain, the clearinghouse he uses to process his trades, he has on a blue-and-yellow plaid shirt, with a dark-blue tie loosely knotted around his neck. Pinned to the right lapel is a yellow rectangular badge, the cherished sign that he is a seat-holder on the Board of Trade.

The trading floor is as big as an airport hangar, and fairly creaks with the hubbub of voices and footsteps. It has something of the air of a circus. Everyone looks terribly excited. At the time, construction of a sizable addition, which will help ease the constant crush, is under way. The floor is covered in badly scuffed black-and-brown linoleum tile of the sort you might find in a tasteless kitchen. The far wall is all windowed, affording a breathtaking view down LaSalle Street—the Bank of Illinois looming on the immediate right, the somber Chicago Federal on the left. The two side walls are adorned with huge electronic boards, not unlike tote boards at a horse track. They serve a similar function, flashing the latest prices in the different commodities, thus disclosing who is a winner, who a loser. Immediately beneath the computerized price boards are what must qualify as the world's biggest blackboards. Before electronics revolutionized price reporting, prices would chatter by Morse code to young clerks, teetering along catwalks high on the wall, who would chalk in the changing numbers by hand, not always getting them right. The big boards remain as backups if the power should happen to go, and clerks still post prices on competing exchanges that might bear on what gets traded here. Far to the right, news dispatches detailing revolutions, weather, and import and export data are culled from more than a hundred countries and every major American city. When a government is toppled in Tanzania or Ethiopia, the first concern of the traders on the floor is not the future well-being of the country's inhabitants, but how this is going to affect grain prices and, by extension, their wallets.

The most tantalizing features of the floor are the seven octagonal wooden "pits," where all of the action is staged. There are pits for soybeans, wheat, corn, oats, iced broilers, soybean meal, and soybean oil. In an adjacent room, known as the South Room, opened only in 1975, are additional pits for gold, silver, plywood, and mortgage interest rates. The hottest contract at the moment is the highly capricious Treasury bond; I hear that traders get in at five in the morning, a full three hours before trading starts in the South Room, and race onto the floor to find themselves a choice position in the pit.

Slightly to the left as you walk toward the middle of the main floor is the soybean pit, the world's biggest commodity pit. Roughly twenty feet on each of its eight sides, it has four scuffed steps to the top and then seven down to the bottom. Traders speak of it in the same sort of reverent, hushed tones as tennis players use to discuss Centre Court at Wimbledon. The pit was immortalized for me by Frank Norris's 1903 novel, *The Pit*, which chronicled the canny maneuverings of Curtis Jadwin, who managed to corner the wheat market briefly, before the grain became too much for him and took him to the brink of ruin. Along the windows, there used to be a cash area, where small bags of samples of the most current shipments of the various grains were available for inspection. Buyers of the cash crops would stop by, pass some corn or wheat through their fingers, and then hurl the stuff onto the floor. Pieces of paper, electronically clicking prices are what excite the boys in the pits these days.

If you want to talk to the really high rollers, I was told over and over again by professionals who traded stocks and options, then go visit some commodity traders. With commodities, I was informed, storied sums of money are made and lost in seconds. You can lose money before you have had a chance to realize you made it. Because of the virtual absence of rules and the opportunities to make a fortune starting with little more than sheer guts, commodity boys like to call their game "the last frontier." The Commodity Futures Trading Commission in Washington attempts to regulate futures trading, but it has justifiably acquired a do-nothing public image and itself admits it can't keep up with its duties, so locals really fancy themselves modern-day cowboys. "A person can't be successful down here if he's not a gunslinger willing to take lots of risk," Stone likes to say. "This isn't the place for a guy who gets a tingle out of playing the slot machines. Guys come down here and think they're prepared, but when they step into the pits they freeze. Especially when they start to lose. You've got to love risks. You have to get high on risks. Otherwise, you might as well be laying grass sod."

Futures trading involves betting on the future—on crops not yet planted, metals not yet mined, animals not yet born. There is reason to believe that there were futures agreements in what is now Ethiopia in 1000 B.C. Historians, though, pinpoint the merchant trade fairs of Renaissance Europe during the eleventh and twelfth centuries as the start of modern futures trading. Dealers would meet with customers and sell goods that would be delivered when the next caravan rumbled through. Such contracts became com-monplace at fairs of the counts of Champagne in the twelfth century. A year-round trading center in England called the Royal Exchange of London was set up in 1570. Elsewhere in the world, there were good-sized futures markets in Jap-anese "rice tickets" from 1600 to 1910. U.S. futures trading got started in the middle of the nineteenth century, with the introduction of "time" and "to arrive" contracts in corn. Chi-cago, where many farms once prospered, was the mother city of futures, and still is the home.

Many of the commodities listed on futures exchanges are items commonly found, in one form or another, in the pan-tries and refrigerators of the typical household: eggs, sugar, potatoes, soybeans, orange juice, boneless beef, cocoa. They can also be what the typical household is built out of, since lumber and plywood are traded on several exchanges. Con-tracts exist in wine vintages. The Board of Trade once even kicked around the idea of trading Scotch whisky futures. In recent years, some of the most fevered action has been in the so-called financial futures, spawned only in 1977, which include such contracts as deutsche marks, Treasury bills, bonds, and Ginnie Maes (a group of mortgages sold as a se-curity). An even newer game, reborn experimentally late in 1982, was options on commodity futures, which had been traded for years until they were outlawed in 1978 because so many crooked dealers were gulling the public.

In brief, a commodity-futures contract is an agreement to deliver a particular commodity at a set price on a fixed date. Though contemporary futures trading often seems to come down to nothing more than a game of dice, the trading of futures came into being as a way to set prices and thus cut the risk for farmers and other producers of commodities. Since a farmer spends most of the year growing his crops, bringing them to market in one fell swoop, his only collateral with lenders consists of unharvested crops that are useless unless there is a way of establishing what their rough worth will be in the future, when they are ready for sale. The answer is futures markets. Well before harvest time, the farmer can contract to sell his crops on a futures exchange. Now banks will lend him money with the contract as collateral while he grows his produce (he is, of course, not entirely out of the woods, since weather disasters could still ruin him). The farmer is known as a "hedger." Any producer troubled about swings in prices can also hedge his commodity. There is always guesswork involved in predicting what prices are going to be like when goods are ready for market. The farmer fattening up his pigs can never be certain what the public's appetite for bacon and pork chops is going to be like some months down the road, so he hedges. Exxon, queasy at the possibility that oil prices will drop, hedges oil. Consumers of commodities also hedge. If General Foods is worried (as General Foods often is) that sugar prices are going to rise steeply in subsequent months and therefore complicate the profit margins on its Raisin Bran and its Kool-Aid, it can buy a futures contract assuring the delivery of the sugar it needs at a future date at today's price. If the price falls rather than rises, then General Foods has made a nasty mistake, and the consumer mustn't be surprised to pay more for Kool-Aid. A "classic hedger" is anyone who takes a position in the futures markets equivalent but opposite to his position in the actual commodity. A grain elevator company, for instance, may worry that the price of all the grain it's storing may dip in the months to come. So it sells grain futures contracts calling for delivery of a quantity of grain equivalent to what it has in its elevators, thereby locking in the price. This is a "classic hedge," because the company has not committed itself in the futures market to more grain than it actually possesses. Lots of big companies hedge in this way. Coca-Cola hedges. Pepsi-Cola hedges. Procter & Gamble hedges. Citibank hedges (financial instruments, rarely sugar or wheat).

The hedgers are one component of the futures game. The other players are the speculators—the private investors and professional traders who buy the contracts and assume the risk from the farmers and corporations. They are in it simply and purely to make money. They couldn't care less about having thousands of gallons of heating oil, or millions of bushels of wheat, or endless cartons of orange juice delivered to them. Yet traders love to regale the uninitiated with stories about some hapless wimp who woke up one morning to a front lawn blanketed with pork bellies, or who had to wade through a few thousand potatoes. The fact is that something like 97 percent of the contracts traded in futures markets are never delivered to their speculative buyers, and if they are, they arrive in the form of warehouse receipts. Basically, commodity trading is a game of buying and selling things the trader never actually owns or cares to own. I have heard the exercise described thus: "You buy what you don't want, sell what you don't got."

It is all a game. Unlike stocks, however, futures is a zero-sum game. At all times, half the market is long and half is short. Every dollar lost by one player is made by another. The lure of playing is that no game is faster: nothing else can return such big profits as quickly as futures. Returns can approach a thousand or even ten thousand percent in a given year—good money even at the casinos along the boardwalk in Atlantic City. The reason money can pour in so fast is the leverage. To buy a contract you generally put up only a margin (a good-faith down payment) of 5 percent of the contract value. Thus a wheat contract valued at ten thousand dollars can be yours for as little as five hundred dollars. The dark side of futures is that you can lose far more than you invest. As your contract dwindles in value, your broker will demand additional margin payments. There is theoretically no limit to what you can lose. There is no bottom to a futures contract. If you sell wheat short and it keeps going up in price, that five hundred dollars you invested can end up costing you twenty or thirty thousand dollars. It is not unlike sitting down at the blackjack table, betting five bucks, losing, and being told you owe thirty.

Until 1972, commodity volume wasn't all that heavy. But the international monetary crisis that year, coupled with a huge increase in world-wide demand for U.S. farm products and the infamous Russian wheat deal, caused futures prices to shoot skyward, and suddenly people who had never heard of the markets before were betting their homes on what was going to happen to March soybeans.

The oldest and biggest active futures exchange in the world, the Board of Trade is the mother church of futures trading. Eighty-two local grain farmers and dealers got together in 1848—the same year that the first telegram was delivered to Chicago and the first shipment of wheat arrived there by rail—and struck a pact to open an exchange where they could sell their corn, oats, and wheat. This was the Board of Trade. Until then, farmers had had to lug their grain from store to elevator in pursuit of buyers. Price fluctuations were extreme. The board's first home was along the banks of the Chicago River, above the Gage and Haines Flour Store. Early records of the board's activities were incinerated in the Great Fire of 1871, though it has become evident that by 1865 the board functioned similarly to the way it does today. Old-timers still recall the days when trade flourished in timothy seed, and hay and oats were brought by traders from horse-drawn trucks and fire wagons. In late 1930, the present forty-four-story building was finished. Today, half of all futures trading goes on at the board, where a whopping twenty-five hundred telephone lines snake into the trading floor alone.

The king-sized digital clock high on the wall reads 9:12, which means there are eighteen minutes till the soybean pit opens for business. Beans start to trade promptly at 9:30 and wind up at 1:15. By my rough count, there are maybe three hundred traders and brokers fanned out on various steps in the pit. Some of the traders look sleepy; others already have that glazed look I have come to know, of a trader running numbers and patterns through his head, puzzling out the strategy that's going to produce paydirt. The assortment of jacket colors is piebald: I spot gold, green, red, black, brown, gray, navy, light blue, dark blue. Each trader clutches a thick stack of order cards in his hand, like a poker player looking for a game.

Where a trader stands, as it happens, has more than casual bearing on his work. By board custom, the outer three steps of the pit are reserved for traders interested in the most active contract, generally the one chronologically closest to hand. The center of the pit is for the second farthest out, and the third most active month is traded on the top step in one corner of the pit. Contracts six or more months down the road exchange hands in another secluded region of the top stair. Such logistical demarcations help traders know where to look, amid the confusion, for prospective buyers and sellers. Within this framework, new traders prowl around for a comfortable spot and then tend to plant themselves there day after day. After a trader finds his spot, it becomes his principality, not to be intruded on by anyone else. Stone, who trades only the most active month, recalls testing several different locations before settling on the third step, at an angle such that his left side is crooked slightly toward the windows overlooking the street. The height of the other traders who stand there suits him well, and he has found that the location affords him a good panorama of the pit.

Nine-thirty. A pit official whacks a rusty gong with a small hammer, and order instantaneously, almost unbelievably, gives way to bedlam. Jostling traders and brokers simultaneously begin to bellow bids at the top of their lungs and as fast as they can move their lips, at the same time that they flail their arms in the air as if they were shooing away killer mosquitoes. Everyone seems to have gone ape. Traders shout into each other's faces, speaking a patois of pit shorthand and abbreviated prices: "Ten July at a quarter." "Five Jans at a half." December is Deece. November is Novee. The din is awesome. It takes a moment or two for my ears to adjust, and it seems unimaginable that anyone can make much sense out of the mumbo-jumbo. Unlike stock exchanges, where specialists umpire the buying and selling, in the pit every commodity trader acts as his own personal auctioneer. There are hardly any rules to abide by. In fact, one trader told me, "There is just one rule, and that is that there are no other rules." All trading is conducted by what is known as "open outcry." No bids are to be made in secret (though, inevitably, some are). Traders simply shout out their offers and then scan the pit for takers, giving no heed to the fact that fellow traders might be in the midst of barking out their own bids. Everyone does his best to speak louder than everyone else. Getting heard in the continuous roar is no easy matter, and there is no way that every bid can be heard by every trader and broker. Public orders, I found out, don't always get executed in the best interests of the public, since the broker is not always as keen on searching through the pit for the best bid as he is on just getting the order out of the way or help-ing a buddy out of a jam. The whole scene is like a dinner party composed of resolutely rude guests who spend the evening interrupting one another.

Frank Norris, attempting to describe a 1900s opening, wrote this passage: "Instantly a tumult was unchained. Arms were flung upward in strenuous gestures, and from above the crowding heads in the Wheat Pit a multitude of hands, eager, the fingers extended, leaped into the air. All articu-late expression was lost in the single explosion of sound as the traders surged downwards to the centre of the Pit, grab-bing each other, struggling towards each other, tramping, stamping, charging through with might and main." In eighty-odd years, things haven't changed much.

The faces of some traders seem to have a demonic cast. Others are flushed with bonhomie. On still others, smiles bloom and fade about as fast as the prices change. Traders and brokers are herded so tightly they can barely do more than jiggle against one another. Each trader searches the pit with querying eyes and concentrative energy, like a radar beam at an airport sweeping the sky for planes. I watch one man with a walrus mustache who, I believe, had a physician been present, would have been singled out for an imminent stroke. Melodrama gets played out in every pit, every day.

From his third-step perch, Stone makes a buy from a lithe, bony-faced man to his right, talking at 2^7 words per second. He makes a hasty notation in a crabbed scrawl on the topmost of a fat stack of cards to be turned in later to his clearinghouse for processing. He sells two contracts to a man on his immediate left who has a racking cough, buys four from across the pit, then becomes passive.

Stone, performing in the pit, is a curious study of widely oscillating emotions and seeming lapses in motor control.

During spells when nothing is being offered that whets his appetite and when he doesn't happen to have anything that he wishes to unload at the prevailing market price, he stands erect, spine straight as a poker, his feet spread apart at a comfortable distance, his arms collapsed across his chest, one hand clutching his deck of trading cards, the other grasping a pencil. His face is stoic. Around him are all these boisterous supplicants. Stone is Cesare Borgia. The pleas rebound off his ears. Then, without warning, a cry reverberates from some corner of the pit that piques his interest, and he seems to undergo a chemical reaction. He starts bobbing up and down, his feet on tiptoe, and both arms shoot high and wide into the air, as if his pants have suddenly caught fire and he is signaling for an extinguisher. He booms out his interest in the offer at a decibel level that approaches, and sometimes seems to exceed, the Rolling Stones' at a rock concert. Once the trade is agreed to orally, he scratches down the pertinent information in a chicken scrawl that a handwriting-analysis group would have trouble deciphering, then eases back into his impassive mode. When fluctuations in prices persuade him to try to dump a contract on someone else, he will sometimes simply stand there with both arms upthrust and one finger on each hand extended, as if he were signaling victory in some obscure war.

Hand gestures, I quickly learn from Stone, are not simply histrionics that traders employ to get attention. The signals matter every bit as much as booming voices in the mayhem of the pits. Each thrashing finger carries specific meaning. The translation of the flying fingers goes like this: A trader who wants to sell holds his palm outward. When he wants to buy, he thrusts it inward. He indicates the quantity that he wants to buy or sell by holding up fingers vertically. One finger signifies one contract (or, in the bean pit, five thousand bushels of beans), two means two, and so on. A January soybean contract, at one moment, was selling for some thirty thousand dollars, so every finger a trader held up stood for thirty grand. ("You really respect a guy once he regularly starts to wave three or four digits in the air," Stone informs me.) If a trader is a "big hitter," as heavy traders are called, and wants to deal in hundreds of contracts, then he crosses one arm over the other before raising his finger. Each finger now represents a hundred contracts, or three hundred thousand dollars' worth of January beans. Needless to say, nobody crosses his arms without due deliberation.

The price you're willing to accept or pay is expressed with horizontally extended fingers. Trading proceeds in movements of at least an eighth of a cent, so one outwardly thrust finger stands for an eighth of a cent. Two fingers mean a quarter of a cent, three signify three-eighths, and four are a half-cent. Five fingers spread apart represent five-eighths of a cent; five fingers squeezed together, three-quarters of a cent. A thumbs-up signal stands for seven-eighths. A closed fist is a full cent. If you're bidding more than a cent, you would hold out one finger on one hand and then the fraction on the other. You have to be fast with the fingers and you have to be explicit. Now and then, deceptions are attempted. I was told of traders who might hold out two fingers on each hand and execute a trade; the other trader thinks he meant two and a quarter, but when he doublechecks with the person, he's told, Not at all, I meant two and was just underscoring it by using both hands. If a trader pulls this once, he's allowed the benefit of the doubt. If he pulls it often, he's known as having "spaghetti fingers." Before long, he's going to be eating nothing better than spaghetti, because nobody will trade with him. The night before they debut on the floor as genuine traders, rookies typically spend laborious hours before a mirror practicing their hand signals, terrified that they'll mess up and buy two million bushels at three-quarters when they wanted to sell five thousand at a cent. As it happens, traders pick up the rhythm of the signals quickly. Besides, the first week they're doing little more than holding up one finger, since they are too jittery and inadequately capitalized to trade more than the absolute minimum.

To keep the electronic prices in sync with the wheeling and dealing on the oak steps, there is a pulpit set off the top stair of the pit in which are stationed several so-called pit reporters. These punch the latest prices into a computer console hooked into the price boards on the wall. The reporters have to keep their eyes glued to the pit, since the traders are supposed to flash them signs every time they complete a trade. During crazy stretches, one of the last things on a trader's mind is getting the price reported, and so, intermittently, one of the reporters will snatch a bullhorn and blurt out a plea: "Gentlemen, please report your prices. Thank you." The usual consequence is that the traders don't start reporting their prices until some peace returns to the pit.

Several basic types congregate in the commodity pits. There are the spread traders, hedging one month against another; the position men, who buy large quantities of a contract and hold it for days, betting on a big move; the day traders, who cling to their positions no longer than a day. Most of the traders, though, are scalpers. They buy and sell hundreds of contracts a day, holding them sometimes for nanoseconds, foraging for a half-cent move here, a quarter-cent there, making their income in dribs and drabs. By the end of the day, they have no position at all, and whatever happens overnight is of no concern to them. It is a trying way to make a living. A scalper often picks up no more than fifteen or twenty dollars on a given trade, so he's got to be constantly in there scavenging, groveling, hunting for every last vestige of profit.

Stone, when he began his trading career, used to predominantly day-trade and position-trade. The way the game goes in these forms of trading, you typically suffer far more losing trades than winning ones, but your winning trades more than cancel out the losers. To be proficient at it, though, you've got to be mentally armored to ride out days or weeks of heavy losses before a trade comes in, like the horse player awaiting the eighty-to-one shot that romps home a winner. Stone used to find his moods swinging dramatically. Any time he had a losing day he would be plunged into a brooding silence. At night, when he got home, his face told his wife exactly what kind of day it had been. More often than not, the look was a sullen one.

It got to be too much. Scalping is a far more even proposition, in which you expect to come home a winner, albeit a smaller winner, four days out of five. So Stone switched to scalping. Like most scalpers, he specializes in just one commodity and just one contract month, the closest at hand. Trading several different months as actively as a scalper needs to trade becomes disconcerting. A single soybean month, though, is quite adequate to reward Stone with an annual take of well into six figures.

"For an average scalper," Stone has often explained when running down his personal rules of scalping, "a couple of hundred dollars up or down would be an average day. A disciplined scalper will not let himself lose much more than that. A good scalper just wants to grind it out and make some money most days. Some days it might only be twenty-five bucks. Other days it might be two hundred. A good average scalper just doesn't want to lose money any days. He loses twenty-five or fifty dollars, that's a bad day. A scalper wants to make money four days and lose one, so he has a net three winners. We have twenty-two trading days a month. If I can make money eighteen or twenty days, I'm a happy man. When I was day-trading, I could have eighteen losers but four winners that more than made up for them. It wouldn't be uncommon for me to make or lose ten thousand dollars in a day. Now a thousand dollars is a great day."

Prices don't have to change much for Stone to flirt with greatness, since one of a commodity trader's perks for being on the floor is that he has to pay only $1.60 in clearing fees to buy and sell a contract, what's called a "round turn." By comparison, John Q. Investor would pay Paine Webber or Merrill Lynch about forty-five dollars for the same thing.

During an average session, Stone will make roughly a hundred individual trades, usually an equal number of buys and sells, since his goal is to be "flat," or without any position, by day's end. A great quantity of the trades will be "scratches," meaning he sells a contract for the identical price he paid for it, simply because no hoped-for profit opportunity materializes. "If I'm cooking," Stone says, "more of the remaining trades will be profitable than unprofitable. Of course, I'm not always cooking."

January beans puddle down seven cents from yesterday's close, then down six and a half cents, then six cents. All this within minutes. Then to five. All the other months are down. This has been a period of bumper crops for grains, coupled with fairly restrained demand, so prices have been eroding steadily. Now January, just five minutes into the trading, is back down six and a half cents. After the fury of the opening, the activity falls to a lower ebb. The blood runs slower.

Stone, arms folded, shifts from foot to foot. He has a habitual sidewise squint, as if he expects assassins around every corner. For the moment, the pit is all but innocent of bids. Stone takes the time to cool his heels. Relaxation can mean thirty seconds out of the pit. One thing commodity traders remember to do is visit the bathrooms before the opening bell since they rarely find the time to get there during trading hours. While resting, traders try to avoid thinking too deeply. Too much thinking gets them into all sorts of trouble and usually causes their most egregious errors. It is the enemy of instinct, which is what traders live by. Thus far, Stone's instinct has been a bit faulty. "See, I bought some beans, and the second I bought them the market went down," he tells me, thumbing through his trading cards. "I didn't like it, so I sold them. I bought a hundred thousand bushels and the price dropped a penny. It cost me a quick thousand dollars. Had I held it, though, I would have been sorry. The market went down another couple of cents. When you realize you're wrong, you get out of the trade and go on to the next one. The most important thing is to get rid of ill-starred trades. I rarely hold anything more than twenty minutes or a half-hour. Usually it's seconds or fractions of a second."

"How much price movement do you need to make a trade worthwhile?" I ask.

"At times, a quarter of a cent," Stone says. "At other times, ten cents. The biggest winner I had so far today was a two-cent winner. The biggest loser I had was a cent and a half. The worst loss I might suffer would be two cents. If I have a really good trade going, I try to wring five or six cents out of it. But generally I try not to make or lose more than a half-cent on a trade. That's five hundred dollars. I don't mind *making* more than five hundred. Losing it tends to upset my stomach."

"You know, I can't tell a thing that's going on in there," I remark. "All I hear is noise."

"I can sit here and tell you exactly where the market is," Stone replies. "I can sit here and tell you not only what the bid is but who's bidding it. You get this from years of pit hearing."

By bean-pit yardsticks, Stone is considered a fairly large scalper. On a typical day, he trades roughly three to four million bushels of beans, mostly in hundred-thousand-bushel swipes. That amounts to twenty contracts. Every trader, over time, arrives at what is a comfortable trading unit for him, above which he starts to get shaky, his blood pressure creeps upward, and he becomes more religious than he ever thought possible. It's all according to how well you feel the pulse of the market and how wide your bank roll is. Some traders have been down on the floor for many years and are still only comfortable trading a solitary contract at a time. Both fat cats and skinny cats prowl the pits.

Traders have different viewpoints on what trading is about. "You have to tell yourself you will trade so much, and you will sell if something goes up so much or down so much," Stone says. "A lot of trading, really the biggest part of trading, is biting the proverbial bullet. It seems that whenever a trader exceeds the limit that he's comfortable with, ninety-nine percent of the time he ends up losing money."

A trader who trades well beyond his accustomed limit is said to be "flipping out." It's a temptation all traders fight from time to time. They catch the scent of what appears to be a ripe opportunity and wonder: Should I go just a little bigger? Should I put a little more on the line?

Not long ago, to drum up public investors, a major commodity-trading firm ran a full-page newspaper advertisement that presented snippets of trading advice assembled from its national network of commodity experts. Among its truisms were these:

> Follow the trends. This is probably some of the hardest advice a trader has to follow, because the personality of the typical futures trader is not "one of the crowd." Futures traders (and futures brokers, I might add) are highly individualistic people. The markets seem to attract these kinds of people.
>
> Keep reminding yourself on every position you take, "my first loss is my least loss."
>
> Do not overstay a good market—you are bound to overstay a bad one also.
>
> Most people would rather own something (go long) than owe something (go short); it's human nature. The markets aren't human. So you should learn that markets can (and should) be traded from the short side.
>
> Establish your trading plan before the opening. This eliminates emotional reactions. Don't change during the session unless you have a very good reason.
>
> Recognize that fear, greed, ignorance, generosity, stupidity, impatience, self-delusion, etc., can cost you a lot more money than the market(s) going against you and that there is no fundamental method (that I know of) to recognize these factors.

Don't blindly follow computer trading. A computer trading plan is only as good as the program. You know the old saying, "Garbage in, garbage out."

Standing aside is a position.

When you go stale, get out of the markets for a while. Trading commodity futures is demanding and can be draining—especially when you're losing. Step back, get away from it all . . . to recharge your batteries.

Don't trade on rumors. If you do, you probably still will. But ask yourself this. "Over the long run, have I made money or lost money trading on rumors?" O.K., then, stop it.

Unlike stocks, which can theoretically go to the moon on a given day or drop in value to a nickel or even nothing, each commodity can vacillate only so much during one session, according to parameters imposed on it by the exchange. Soybeans can rise or fall no more than forty cents over the previous day's settlement price (the final averaged closing price). A bean contract that advances the full forty is said to be "up-limit." If it drops forty, it has gone "down-limit." The limits help restrict the number of gallons of blood spilled on the floor, and also allow brokerage houses some breathing time to round up additional margins from investors whose positions have taken nasty turns. A forty-cent move doesn't sound like much until you do the arithmetic, but it amounts to two thousand dollars for every soybean contract. If you happened to own a hundred contracts, you're talking about two hundred thousand dollars. Limit moves are something a trader learns to live with. In volatile markets, they happen frequently and they happen fast—sometimes within a couple of minutes of the opening gong. Limit moves can cause bone-chilling moments or waves of ecstasy, depending on whether they are in your favor or not. If you're short and the market double-crosses you and goes up-limit two or three days in a row without giving you a chance to cover your position, as it's been known to do on infrequent occasions, the feeling is just about heart-stopping. "Like sinking in quicksand," Stone says. "You're as helpless as a newborn baby. There's not a blessed thing you can do. Some traders cry."

One thing to do is avoid getting in too deeply to begin with. "The most I'll ever take on one trade is maybe four hundred thousand bushels," Stone tells me. "The guy standing next to me I've seen take five hundred thousand to a million beans on a trade."

I ponder that. "Sounds risky," I say.

"Yeah," Stone murmurs. "Way too risky. You're talking about ten thousand dollars on a penny. The market moves a penny, you're talking about ten thousand dollars made or lost. That can happen like this—" He snaps his fingers and vanishes back into the noisy pit.

During the torrid course of the trading, young, fresh-faced male and female "runners" dart back and forth into the pit. Their mission is to deliver to pit brokers order slips that have been called in to phone clerks. Brokers, once they execute an order, deposit the slip on an outer step of the pit for the runner to retrieve. For instance, I notice that Louis W. Ritten & Co. has bought five Jans for somebody and Heinold Commodities has picked up five Marches. I also notice that, before orders get scooped up, they inevitably get marred with footprints from being stepped on.

It is thirty minutes later. Stone climbs out of the pit for a quick breather and he plops down on a bench set on the top step, scratching his scalp with his finger. He looks a little mopey. "Here's a potential problem," he says, nodding at one of his trading cards. "I sold one lot of beans and I have no idea who I sold it to. I made three trades—bang, bang, bang. I remember two, but the third person didn't come back to me to double-check it. I sold it short, so if I don't cover and the market closes higher I'm screwed."

"How much would you lose?" I ask.

"Seven thousand dollars."

"So how are you going to decide what to do?"

"Guess."

Hoisting himself up to get ready to trudge back into the pit, Stone smiles thinly. "Every time you take a trade, you don't know if you're going to make money or lose money," he says. "So that's why the physical strain is so great, why the mental and emotional pressure is so tremendous. Maybe we don't work long hours or get our hands dirty, but we make more decisions in a four-hour day in that pit than the average person makes in a year."

Malapropos as it seems, a trader whose entire livelihood is reliant on the bean pit often knows next to nil about the product that he or she is feverishly buying and selling by thousands of bushels. When I ask Stone about this one afternoon he smiles and replies, "I think you could probably walk in here with a soybean plant and twenty-five to fifty percent of the traders wouldn't know what the hell it was." As it happens, Stone has been acquainted with the soybean, and he does, in passing, follow news about the bean, though it is not vital to his work. As a means of sustenance, though, soybeans don't particularly turn him on. "Roasted soybeans are all right," he has said. "But to me, they're kind of blah. But there's very little today that we eat that doesn't have soybeans in it."

Yet the average pit scalper neither eats the bean nor knows anything about it? I ask.

"Wouldn't know or wouldn't care," he says.

Too bad, actually. It's a curious bean. Though it took a long while getting there, it is now America's number-one cash crop, having surpassed wheat and then corn. Four thousand years ago, it was one of the five sacred grains of China. Unlike us, the Chinese gobble up tons of soybean curd (calling it "meat without bones"). It's a legume that will grow just about anywhere that corn or cotton will. Thirty states harvest the beans. Illinois is the top producer, chased by Iowa. When young, the soybean plant is a lush green, three feet high, with broad leaves. Fully ripe, it looks like a pitiful weed. The bean doesn't look like much, either. It's a pale-yellow pellet. The shell is hard and must be crushed to produce meal and oil. The meal is fed to livestock and poultry, or refined into flour. The oil goes into cooking oil, salad oil, margarine, and shortening. A puny amount also goes into things like paint, soap, printers' ink, and cements. Fish meal is competitive with soybean meal on the world market, so bad news for fish meal is good news for soybeans. In 1973, when fish mysteriously disappeared off the coast of Peru, bean exports rose by fifty million bushels and prices soared. The fish, however, eventually came back.

Though you may not require encyclopedic knowledge (or even a passable dictionary definition) of what you trade, a commodity trader had better be able to look out for himself. Futures is the most physically grueling type of trading. It can get downright brutal. In the bean pit, scrapes and bruises are common from all the pushing and elbowing. One trader yanked up his pants leg and showed me a welter of black-and-blue marks he got from being kicked. It looked as though he had been assailed by the Hell's Angels. Somebody else told me that his ribs have been sore for years and he once mulled over the idea of donning a corset. One of the reasons so few women flail away in the pits is the physical toll the work takes. What's more, most women are just too short to have good pit visibility, though one edge they do have is their distinctive high-pitched voices. Years ago, many brokers used to require women customers to get the written consent of their husbands before taking the women on, under the belief that women were less capable than men of standing the emotional strain of futures markets.

Other occupational hazards of pit trading include varicose veins, flat feet, sore backs, hoarse throats, ulcers, weak hearts, and high blood pressure. Falls from the steep stairs are not unknown. Miscarriages occur. A staff of six paramedics work at the board to handle such incidents as heart attacks, strokes, stabbings from sharp pencils. The last death on the floor, the medical staff reports, was a clerical worker felled by a coronary in 1978. But not even death stops the trading in the pits.

One trader tells me that hemorrhoids are a fairly common malady. "It used to be the barber's disease," he cheerily informs me. "Now it's the commodity trader's disease. We're on our feet all day, standing on those hard boards. So you get hemmies." The ears take a pounding, too. Some traders pop aspirin to dull the roar of the pits. Others stuff their ears with cotton. I encounter a corn trader who swears by industrial earplugs that are supposed to block out high frequencies but let in the middle ranges. Several guys in the bean pit have permanently lost something like 80 percent of their voices from too many years of screeching. One all-but-voiceless trader remains active. His vocal level is little above a whisper. You have to pay special attention to his hand signals, which have become exceptionally precise, and try to read his lips.

Stone, who pumps three to four miles a day on an exercise bike to keep his body trim, has had high blood pressure since he was a kid. It seemed pretty well under control until a year ago, when it took a sharp rise. He embarked on a salt-free diet, which he still sticks to, and his pressure has settled down. Other than that, he has avoided anything more serious than a bruise here and there. "I got an elbow in the stomach yesterday," he tells me. "Pencils get me every so often. Occasionally, I get kicked. That's about all." Like all traders, he has witnessed a lot worse. As he describes it, "I've seen a couple of heart attacks in the pit. One was mild and one was pretty severe. He was no more than forty and is no longer trading. Actually, he shouldn't have been here in the first place. He had the wrong mental attitude. There was another guy who went home, didn't feel well, and dropped dead of a heart attack. He was in his late forties. One guy had a heart attack and a triple bypass operation and, believe it or not, he's still trading. I honestly don't know what motivates him. I'd be scared shitless."

The mental toll on commodity traders is also great. This point is driven home by the case of Philip Hehmeyer. Hehmeyer was a big cotton trader on the New York Cotton Exchange who had been making good money for a decade. His furious trading style got him the nickname of "Haywire." When things really started cooking in the pits, Hehmeyer would don a black visored cap outfitted with red blinking lights. He lived the good life. He tooled around in an antique Jaguar, went tarpon fishing off the Florida coast, sipped Dom Perignon when the market was good. Then, according to those who knew him, he started to get despondent about the state of the economy and the markets he traded. One Monday in August 1982, he dropped about sixty-four thousand dollars trading cotton. He made some money trading gold that Thursday, but then he lost almost sixty thousand guessing wrong on the Standard & Poor stock-index futures. That night, he bolted the door of his posh Upper East Side apartment, got out the shotgun he used to hunt geese, and blew his brains out. He was thirty-seven and supposed to be married in two weeks.

Individuals from every conceivable background seem to become commodities traders. During my various pilgrimages to the floor of the Board of Trade, I often heard about Eugene Cashman, a cop whose beat included the streets around the board building. He wandered in one day, looked things over, got the bug, and shucked his blue uniform for a red trading smock. Cashman called the bullish 1973 bean market correctly and made the kind of money princes dream about in fairy tales. Interested in aping his success, a number of fellow officers of the law decided to trade risk of life for risk of bankruptcy, and descended into the pits. Any number of former Chicago athletes now do their blocking in the board pits. I ran across several ex–Chicago Cubs, most notably Glenn Beckert, the talented Cubs second baseman, who was fielding wheat contracts, and a few ex–Chicago Bears, such as former tackle George Seal. They were at least used to being physically pummeled. One morning, I encountered a person I hadn't seen for years, a former reporter in the Chicago bureau of *The Wall Street Journal*. A few years back, he had come into a tidy family inheritance and decided to see what he could do with it in the fastest game in town. I ran across ex-stockbrokers, ex-plumbers, ex–train conductors, ex-lawyers, ex-doctors (including a former brain surgeon), ex–cab drivers, ex–advertising executives, and an ex-teacher of handicapped children. I got the feeling that the rest of the professional world was nothing more than a massive training camp for a career as a commodity trader. I heard about a lawyer in his mid-forties who was an addicted gambler. He played the ponies. He bet football games. His practice, meanwhile, slid downhill. In desperation, he tried Gamblers Anonymous. He was less anonymous but no more cured. Finally, he decided to chuck the bar and pursue his inclination. He bought a seat on the Board of Trade.

Stone certainly never plotted in advance to spend 9:30 to 1:15 each weekday taxing his lungs in the soybean pit. He was born in 1954 in Chicago, where his father was a prosperous Chicago real-estate magnate. When Stone went off to Tulane University he had little notion what career path he would take. After one semester at Tulane, he dropped out, disgruntled with the school, and returned to Chicago, where he found a job selling sporting goods. One fateful day, he bumped into a distant cousin who ran a clearinghouse on the Chicago Mercantile Exchange, the country's second-biggest commodities marketplace. One of the cousin's runners had just quit, and so he inquired whether Stone might want to fill the spot. Stone knew absolutely zip about futures, only that his own was uncomfortably aimless, and so he decided to give it a whirl. He got $75 a week for the lowest job in the floor's pecking order. Though called "runners," they were sternly instructed to *walk* orders to brokers. In moments of panic, though, Stone remembers "walking at a hurried pace."

To be a good runner, you needed some of the traits of a Gale Sayers. Many traders evolve from runners, for if one comes down to the floor of a big exchange and witnesses all the excitement and hears all the talk of millions being made, why, how can one resist? The floor has an inexorable draw.

At once, Stone was intoxicated by the milieu. "I saw everyone yelling and screaming, and it just fit my personality to a tee. The place was wonderful. It was a magic kingdom."

Working diligently, Stone was promoted to phone clerk after about six months. He stuck with that for a year, then decided to return to college and eventually come back to the exchange as a trader. He got a degree in agricultural economics at the University of Illinois. The summer before he finished college, just after turning twenty-one, he acquired some seasoning at the MidAmerica Commodity Exchange, which looms across the street from the Board of Trade and is a sort of minor league for futures trading, where a good many Board of Trade habitués cut their teeth doing shoestring trading. At the MidAmerica, the basic trading unit is one-thousand-bushel contracts, as opposed to the five-thousand minimum at the Board of Trade. Thus for each penny movement in your favor at MidAmerica, you pocket ten dollars, whereas at the Board of Trade you make fifty bucks. "I figured that if I was going to make a lot of mistakes as a beginner, as beginners do, then I was going to do it at ten dollars a shot rather than fifty," Stone recalls. It's sort of like playing the two-dollar blackjack table before tackling the five-dollar one.

That summer, Stone had a reservoir of roughly two thousand dollars to risk. "I damn near broke even for the month and a half I was down there. I traded corn, one thousand bushels at a time—no more. Corn traded in one-quarter-point ticks, so if it moved a quarter of a cent in the right direction I earned two dollars and fifty cents. A big day for me was twelve-fifty. I think the greatest day I had was twenty bucks. The worst day was a twenty-five-dollar loss." But he picked up invaluable tutelage. "As a trader, you have a lot of fears. I got many of those early jitters worked out. I learned market feel—how to get a feel for when the market is going up or down. It's tough to put into words how you do it, but it has to do with noise and who's trading how much. You have to know if the boys in the pits are long or short. If they're long, the market is likely to break. If the boys are short, then they're going to have to cover their positions and the market is going to rally." Finally, in January 1977, armed with his college degree and his skimpy trading experience, Stone bought a Board of Trade seat.

It really doesn't take all that much to get down in the pits. It's not necessary to prove any deep comprehension of the commodity markets or of whatever specific items you plan to trade. All you need are two sponsoring members and enough knowledge to be able to pass a not especially taxing exam on the mechanics of trading. The FBI makes sure you have no criminal record. The SEC checks that you have committed no securities fraud. The main bête noire is the price of the seat. The going rate then was a hundred and twenty-five thousand dollars. A board seat sold for three hundred and twenty-five thousand in 1980 (the last sale, in mid-1983, was two hundred and fifty-one thousand) and as little as twenty-five bucks during the Second World War, when the government clamped tight restrictions on grain prices and the pits were practically dead. There are still a couple of traders on the floor who got their seats at the twenty-five-dollar rate. One of them had to borrow money to do it.

Traders will do just about anything, short of a Brinks'-type robbery, to get the cash to buy a board seat. I learned about one particularly resourceful and daredevil man named George Koehl, who, back in the early 1900s, worked as a Western Union messenger boy at the Board of Trade. In 1911, he decided he wanted to become a trader. He needed around twelve hundred bucks for a seat. He possessed six hundred. Casting his fate to the long ball, he bet the entire sum on the upcoming World Series, taking the Philadelphia Athletics over the New York Giants at even-money odds. He won, and went on to make millions trading wheat, remaining a member for fifty-three years, right up until his death at age seventy-four. His grandson, who works in public relations at McDonald's and who related all this to me, told me, "He had an incredible mathematical mind. He was the type of guy you could ask to multiply three digits by three digits and he would give you the answer faster than you could do it by pencil." He was nimble, too. In his grandson's words: "He used to move around in those damned pits like grease." The grandson said that he used to go down to the pits with his grandfather, and he noticed that in his waning years he would periodically ask him to recite the prices on the big chalkboards: he was going blind and was using his grandson as his eyes. One dark day, Koehl lost a million dollars in the pits. Anxious about telling his wife when he got home, he finally just blurted it out: "Honey, I lost a million dollars today." She hardly changed her expression and said, "Well, George, let's go in for dinner."

As for his own prospective seat, Stone had nothing like a hundred and twenty-five grand, so, like many traders, he took out a bank loan, guaranteed by his father's mammoth investments. His parents might be described as less than ebullient about his choice of callings. "I think my father might have preferred me to be a doctor or a lawyer or an accountant," Stone has said, "what the world perceives as being more professionally oriented. But I think he realized that if I were successful in this business, I could be more successful at an earlier age than in anything else. The only restriction as to how much you make is how good you are. I guess we both felt that I had the self-discipline and understood capital management well enough to be a good trader. I think those two things are the key to survival down here."

Eight hundred dollars a month was what Stone needed to pay off the loan on his seat. In the beginning, he lived at home, so his expenses were close to nil. But his father made it clear that the loan was his nut. Stone had a lot of nervous moments. "When I started, I didn't know if I could make a dollar." He began as an order-filler, as brokers are known. They generally get $1.50 for each order they execute. At that rate, you have to fill a tall stack of orders to make decent money. And there are the inevitable errors ("outtrades" in the lexicon of the floor), which seem to haunt rookie brokers as fumbles plague a new running back. Brokers, Stone figures, wind up shelling out between 15 and 20 percent of their grosses on outtrades. You read a sell order as a buy, a buy as a sell. You might spot a trader holding up what looks like four fingers. He actually has all five up, but the thumb is hidden behind the others.

Stone stuck with brokerage work for three years, squeezing in trading for himself when he had the chance. One day he was handed an order that, as he recalls, "caused my heart to go bang, bang, bang. I think I must have turned white." It was for five million bushels. Executing it meant fifteen hundred dollars. His happiest day, however, was July 14, 1980, his birthday, when the market delivered a present in the form of an up-limit move while Stone was flush with contracts. He earned enough money in that one day to pay off the balance of the loan on his seat.

The occasional big order notwithstanding, brokerage is a constant hustle and you are never the master of your own destiny. Plus you can't make the money possible for a good trader on his own. So, his confidence finally at the appropriate vertiginous level, in late 1980 Stone switched to full-time trading for himself, and has never looked back. Stone's wife, whom he met one day in the laundry room at college, is perhaps more understanding of the chronic ups and downs of the profession than most wives (traders tend to go through marriages and relationships as quickly as they go through money), since she is a trader of sorts herself. Both her father and brother were members of the Chicago Mercantile Exchange, and so her degree in advertising was applied not to singing the virtues of floating soap but to buying and selling Treasury bills on the Merc floor. Health problems, however, ruled out her continuing in the pits, and now she trades from their Chicago condominium. Channel 26 broadcasts commodities and stock prices throughout the morning hours. She sits riveted before the TV, watching the river of numbers float down the screen. She plots elaborate charts of past price behavior. When everything looks absolutely ripe, and the lines are going the right way, she pounces—she picks up the phone and buys or sells. Her trading unit has been established beyond any conceivable doubt: she trades one contract at a time and makes roughly one trade a month.

"There are guys who make a million dollars and there are guys who lose a million dollars," Stone is telling me during a break from the pits. Stories about making and losing money are usually primary in a trader's arsenal of smalltalk. "I can tell you about a guy who a year ago this week was up a million and a half. Four weeks later, on January first, he was out three hundred thousand for the year. He lost a million eight in the month of December."

How did the trader take it? I ask.

"Not well," Stone says. "Massive depression. I'll tell you, if I ever gave back a million, then gave back another million on top of that, I'd go blow my brains out."

Traders who go bust are said, in floorese, to "tip out." Thus, it is not uncommon to hear such a comment as "Hey, guess what, Horace just tipped out" or "I knew it was coming. Dwight just tipped." Tippers suffer from many flaws, though the most prevalent ones tend to be a lack of discipline and an inability to read a market. Bad traders are known for "chasing a market," buying into a market that has already rallied or fallen significantly. Nine out of ten times, it's a lousy idea, because the market will start to turn back the other way and you'll be paying out losses. In conversations on the floor, you also hear other words and phrases— like "suck some gas," "give it back," "go in the dinger," "get blown out," "puke out," "take a heavy hit"—meant to signify that a trader made some bad moves.

According to one Board of Trade survey, two out of three commodity traders fail to last ten years in the business. When I ask Stone about the mortality rate for a pit trader, he says, "Of guys starting out, maybe one out of five survives five years. The rest either don't make enough money or they tip out."

"Then what?"

"I don't know," Stone says. "I suppose they drive cabs. Maybe they become muggers."

I leave Stone and wander up to the fifth-floor visitors' gallery, where members of the general public can walk in off the street and peer through glass at the pandemonium below. A few dozen people are milling about, a number of them looking aimlessly at displays of bar graphs documenting the explosive growth of commodity futures: board volume has zoomed up more than eightfold in the last decade. Other visitors smile benignly down on the floor, shaking their heads in awe and bemusement. Historical pictures adorn one wall: a look at the Board of Trade baseball team of

1911; the main trading floor in 1900; a lunchroom order scribbled on a drawing of the building that housed the exchange in the late 1880s—the order was for one boiled ham on white (no butter), one pumpkin pie, and a hot pork on rye with tomato.

There is a series of pictures of cows eating grain, a warehouse, an elevator, and a woman in glasses with her hair tied in a bun who is buying two packages of chopped meat at a shiny supermarket. The accompanying text reads: "Agricultural products require several processing and merchandising steps before they are ready for your grocer's shelves. Hedging on the futures markets allows agribusinesses to reduce the risks of adverse price change. The result is a more efficient marketing system which contributes toward the lowest possible costs to consumers." A debatable statement, since it has never been entirely clear what effect the futures markets have on the price of a loaf of bread or a cotton shirt. Some people think futures drain money from capital formation. Some say it feeds inflation, others that it dampens inflation. No one really knows for sure. But of course this is the exchange talking and this is the exchange line all the way.

A videotape is flickering in the corner of the gallery, and a bunch of people commingle around it, soaking up the information. "It looks like total bedlam," a baritone-voiced announcer intones. "It's actually more organized than it seems. What you're looking at is one of the most primitive forms of bargaining there is. . . ." A floor trader is asked by the announcer to explain the cryptic hand signals. He gives all the right answers, and then he adds a signal not taught in commodity manuals. "Some guys go like this," he says as he clasps his open palms together. "Of course they're praying." To underscore the point, the interviewer adds that on this day on the floor, two gold traders made one too many bad trades and tipped out.

I move away and stare down at the seven pits. Soybean meal and soybean oil are slow, but everything else is percolating. A brigade of teen-agers and an elderly couple are pressed against the windows, eyes agog. The activity is heating up as closing time nears. "I've been to see the air-traffic controllers at O'Hare and that was absolute bedlam," the old woman cackles to her husband. "But I think this takes the cake."

"Like a giant crap game," the husband says, and he dissolves into merriment.

I forge my way down to the floor to witness the day's close. January beans are now down sixteen and a half cents, but to state any price is really to be hopelessly imprecise, because the current figure is vacillating so wildly that it seems to settle at a new level every tenth of a second. Activity is heavier than at any time today, since most of the scalpers are scrambling to get out of positions in these last few minutes so they don't have to hold them overnight, as the position players will, and worry about losing money on tomorrow's opening.

Arms flailing, Stone is trading madly. When the one-minute warning bell sounds, he looks as if he had recently been stabbed with a bayonet and wishes the ambulance would get there soon. His smock is darkened with sweat. With five seconds to go, the noise reaches its peak. More trades get made in the final minute than in any five-minute period in the day. At last, the final bell sounds; the din tapers off. Traders and brokers check final trades, and then there's a slow dispersal from the pit. After the close, many traders, especially those with losing days, make a beeline for a nearby watering hole, to find solace in a Scotch straight up or a bourbon over ice. Others repair to health clubs to work out the kinks and frustrations in a game of racquetball or squash. One trader told me that at the end of most days he felt as if he had just gotten through substituting as a punching bag for Ken Norton.

Having checked out his last-moment transactions, Stone gives me a capsule summary of his final hour in the pit: "When I left you I made one trade that I really got murdered on. I sold a hundred bushels and the market rallied a penny and a half and I covered. That cost me about fifteen hundred dollars. Then I waited and the market broke again. With ten seconds to go, someone offered two hundred and fifty beans. I took a hundred and fifty of them and I got out with a second to go. I made three trades and made half a cent to a penny, so I broke even on the close. I made some money on the day. I can't really complain—I got through another day in the pits and I took some money out."

A few days later, I speak with the Ice Man, a fellow bean trader and close buddy of Stone's. A tall man of thirty-nine with penetrating green eyes and a certain *joie de vivre* about him, he earned his nickname by his uncanny ability to show no perceptible change of demeanor, whether he has just dropped a small fortune or made a haul. He always seems utterly composed. Around the pits, he is known as a "big hitter" who is fond of massive, desperate plunges. Five or ten contract trades are not his speed; he scrambles for fifty or a hundred contracts at one swipe, and seven or eight million bushels of beans pass through his hands on just an average day in the pits. The Ice Man has been blessed with astounding market feel. He relies on intestinal intuition for the undulations of the market to guide him on when to buy and when to sell. He thumbs his nose at recommended practices and gets away with it, like a blackjack player who keeps drawing on sixteen. He hates to "cut and run," and so clings to losing positions longer than conventional wisdom would dictate. He loves to "fade" the boys in the pits—do the opposite of whatever they're doing. His trading career has been one of considerably fluctuant behavior. He has seen millions come and go in a few brief sessions of trading. He tells me about losing a sum, in one fateful morning, that would satisfy an oil man for a year. He tells me about dropping close to two million bucks in another miserable three-day span. He remembers it like a surreal nightmare that will never cease to haunt him.

The Ice Man's real name is Chuck Wafer. He grew up in Denver, the son of a plumbing contractor who, when he wasn't installing pipe, liked to wager on football games and on the ponies, enjoying mixed success. Wafer went off to the University of Colorado, where he developed into a nationally ranked handball player. After a year he got married, and had two kids right away. He soured on formal education shortly afterward. "Going to college with kids and not participating in the college life, I figured I might as well get on with my life. I might as well get on in the world of business." He returned home and signed on in his father's business, digging ditches and putting in pipe. His older brother toiled alongside him. One thing Wafer picked up from his father was his thirst to gamble. He recalls betting many a paycheck on the horses. Laying pipe, though, didn't seem like much of a future to him, and he cast about for something else to do with his life. He still played a lot of handball, and one of his regular opponents was a hotshot at the brokerage firm of

Bache and Company. One fortunate day in 1969, this man offered him a job. Soon after, Wafer became a Bache stockbroker in Denver. When the stock market sank into the doldrums in late 1969, he started to switch people into commodities. He liked the risks, the excitement, the fast action. Before long, Hayden Stone offered him a job to run their Denver office. Soon Continental Grain wooed him away and steered him into commodities in a major way. His sights, however, were set on trading for himself.

"If I was going to stay awake nights worrying about money, and if it was going to eat away at me, I'd rather it be my money," he tells me. "I hated calling people and telling them that they had lost ten thousand dollars and needed two thousand more to bring their account up. That killed me. I began to realize that I had to get on the Board of Trade myself if I ever wanted to get where I wanted to be. I knew that to make the big dough I had to get on that floor."

He finally breezed into Chicago in the spring of 1974, going to work for the Hornblower brokerage firm. They bought him a seat on the board, and Wafer ran their floor operations. For two years he kept the job, fitting in some personal trading when he found time, squirreling away future stakes. In January 1977, he bought a seat and struck out on his own. He played it big from the start. "I've always had a personality of wanting to get ahead," he tells me. "I knew a very successful guy when I was a little kid and I asked him once what made him so successful. He said that you can go from point A to point B by walking, or you can get from point A to point B by running. If you run, you're going to fall down a few times, but you're still going to get there a lot faster. That's always been my philosophy. I know I'm going to have my ups and downs, but I'm going to get places faster than others."

In the first couple of months, he ran up winnings of fifty thousand dollars and wondered where commodities had been all his life. Before much longer, he was ten thousand dollars in the hole. From then on, the dollars got bigger and the roller coaster got wilder. Wafer quickly came to know six- and seven-figure years—on both the plus and the minus sides. In 1980, he was close to a million dollars ahead of the game, before two dark days in June when he gave back two-thirds of it. A bean rally had begun because of a drought in Texas. No beans are grown in Texas, but many speculators were betting that the dry spell was going to invade the bean states. Wafer huffed at that thinking. He stayed short beans. The drought spread to Arkansas and Missouri. Too late, Wafer finally believed. Refusing to knuckle under, he came back with another dazzling ascent. From June until November that year, he went on a roll, winning back his losings and advancing, as he puts it, "seven figures ahead of the game." The reward of the hard work didn't last long. He lost nearly two million of it in three December days, when the bean market deflated like a flat tire. Still, Wafer said he made money for the year, though he suffered a brutal psychic bruising: "I felt like such a fool to lose all that money." This year, still reeling from his disaster, he was down a huge amount between January and April. He told himself just to calm down and try to recoup his losses. At the time I speak with him, in mid-December, he is about even.

"When we have good markets, I love the pits," he tells me. "I love the action. There's nothing more exciting or more stimulating."

How he got through some of the big losses, he doesn't entirely know. I question him about last December's debacle.

"Beans had broken a dollar," he says dryly, with little

trace of remorse. "I was up in Aspen skiing. There was no snow, so I started trading. I bought a million beans and they broke down the limit. I bought another million beans the next day and they went down the limit again. The market just went wacko. It was the next day before I could unload. For the three days, beans went down a dollar. Unfortunately, I had two million beans."

At first he was anesthetized. Then he sank into despair, berating himself for botching things and breaking one of his cardinal rules—never trade sizable positions when you're not in the pits and able to smell the flow of the market.

"They're tough to deal with in a lot of ways," he continues, meaning the losses. "The thing I've found with my style of trading—position trading—is that you can trade good for six months and do well, and then in two or three days they take it all away from you. Then you go another six months trading real good, and they take it all away again in two or three days."

He is pensive for a moment, as if musing to see whether there is still some way to rectify his dreadful mistake.

"It's like when someone dies," the Ice Man says. "The shock is there but you don't really realize it in the couple of days after it happens, because you're scrambling for your life. But then you have to deal with it for six months or so. It gnaws away at you for just months and months. It's like a car that sinks into a lake. It's okay at first, but then it slowly corrodes until it's just a junk. You talk to yourself. I learned over the years that you get upset and you bum out other people around you, and so I try not to spill my troubles on others. Now people don't know if I've had a good day or a bad day, even if it's a real travesty.

"I've seen a guy be up one million and go deficit one million," he goes on. "It's tough. Some guys become a little more low-profile. Maybe you booze it up at night, but you deal with it. A lot of guys drink. I never drank too much. When I would get murdered, I'd leave the board and go play racquetball and handball. Sports was my release."

Though he has several times flirted with ruin, Wafer has never been entirely wiped out. He has never forfeited a house or a car. At times, though, largesse from fellow traders has been necessary to keep him in the pits. "The greatest thing about the Board of Trade is the way the guys help you out. When I first started, I had guys come up to me and give me twenty thousand dollars, but they had to ask me my last name. I couldn't borrow that kind of money then from all the people I knew in Denver." Once, he was forced to borrow three hundred thousand bucks from the bank at a rate of 9.25 percent. Within four months, the rate had ballooned to 22 percent. When he went bad, Wafer would cut back in pica-yune ways. "There were periods when I couldn't fly any-where, when I had to sit down with my family and tell them we had to spend less on food. It's amazing how meticulous I can get when I go bad. I traipse around turning off light bulbs and stupid things like that that aren't even going to matter. But you get scared. I'm still scared. I'm always run-ning scared."

Wafer has at least had the foresight when he is on winning streaks to yank some money out of his trading account and entrust it to safer nests. He tells me he has put money into land, the stock market, oil deals, apartment houses in Den-ver, a house in Chicago, another in Aspen.

Through all the good fortune and the exhilaration of pro-digious runs of luck, though, he has remained humble. "You know that the market can take it from you at any moment. The market keeps you very humble. You know the damned place can take it from you any time it wants to."

Wafer's brother now sells real estate in Denver. He is nothing like Wafer. If he loses five dollars betting on a football game, he is completely crushed, practically incapable of getting through the rest of the day. He has begged Wafer to give up the pits. Wafer's parents have pleaded with him to get out before he gives all the money back one final time. Wafer now steers clear of the floor some five months of the year; he goes skiing, does other things. But the seductions are too strong for him to leave the pits for good. However far away he gets, he still hears their siren song.

"I've thought about getting out of the business," he tells me. "Oh, boy, have I ever. I've cut down my exposure in the last year because of the risk factor. I don't want to give it all back. You know, when you have nothing, things don't bother you so much. As you grow older, you really don't have the stomach to give it back. I think I'm burned out a little. I remember when I started I used to wish the markets were open Saturday and Sunday. I was bored on the weekends. But it's still the kind of thing where I go out to Aspen on vacation and I say to myself I'm not going to trade. I don't care what goes on in those pits, I'm not trading. Sure enough, before you know it I'm on the phone and I'm trading. The bottom line is, what else would I do? Am I going to sell vacuum cleaners and hope I make some good deals and earn thirty thousand dollars? I mean, what's the big deal? How can that excite me? I can go down into that pit and make that in one day."

"If you ask me, those guys are all nuts," a young ponytailed female runner tells me the next day. "They're absolutely crackers. Hang around a trader too long and, I'm telling you, your brain begins to decay." We're standing outside the bean pit, awaiting the opening gong. While we wait, I watch in horror as a gangly runner, too hasty to get an order to a broker, trips over the top step and tumbles into the pit. He quickly picks himself up and, wincing in pain, delivers the order and straggles out of the pit, barely drawing an arched eyebrow from anyone. A spindly trader from another pit plucks at my arm, offers a calloused handshake, and entertains me with a story that does little to disprove that female runner's supposition that pit traders are different from you and me.

Telling stories is one of the floor's chief recreations. Starring in them is the other. "This story involves three guys, including me," the man begins, barely able to contain his mirth. "We're all successful traders, doing the meats and financials then. So one day these two guys, who were my best friends in the business, say, Let's meet for lunch. So I say, Okay, and we're supposed to meet at some gin mill at one-thirty. I showed up and waited for two hours and they didn't come. I got drunk as a bastard and drove home. I went to bed. The following morning, at four A.M., the phone rang and this drunkard is on the other end and he says, Sorry we're late for lunch, join us for breakfast. Where are you? I say. Las Vegas, he says. So I figure what the hell, and I caught the nine o'clock flight out there, being the friend that I am. That night we lose a bundle in the casino, and since we were on a complimentary deal with free food, we decided to get it back the next day by eating like pigs in our room while we watched the Oklahoma-Texas game. We all had some dough riding on it. That night we went to this Chinese joint and we ate like pigs. By now, we had had maybe two or three hours of sleep. We're tired. So I said, Let's take a cab. They said, Let's walk. It was five miles to the hotel—the Tropicana. So we walked. We stopped at every gambling joint between there and the Tropicana, on both sides of the street. We lost enough in that walk throwing dice to buy two limousines and five cabs. The thing about all this is that we get all the action we can get down here, but we still do that. You see, this is your living. There it's a relaxation. It's a release. We're professional commodity speculators. We're not professional dice throwers. By the way, this is not an atypical story."

After a few days of standing in the soybean pit, I begin to pick up distinctive voices, if not actually to discern what everyone is shouting. There is a coarse voice from the left side that goes almost nonstop. There is a high, piercing voice from the center and a raspy one at the far left. A serrated baritone erupts from just beneath the top step.

Stone is standing just outside the bean pit, telling me that it's important for scalpers to close their ears to rumors. He doesn't want to be affected by them. Anything and everything gets suggested. The President's been shot. The President has shot the Vice-President. Russian destroyers are plowing toward the coast of Maine. The United States has invaded China. The United States has invaded the Board of Trade. Soybeans are being laced with poison. An A-bomb has been exploded. Wheat fields are on fire. A story that enters innocently at one end of the floor changes complexion by the time it reaches the other. A trader might inform another trader that his girlfriend has cut her lip. That story might eventually wend its way to the plywood pit, where it by now has been translated into the news that the head of the Federal Reserve has had a massive stroke and may not last the day. Rumors, if they have even feeble plausibility, can drive prices up and down, especially if enough of the big position players swallow them, but most rumors draw no more than knowing nods. "There are just too many wacky stories for me to care," Stone says. "I just watch what goes on in the pit."

An older broker—I would guess his age to be about fifty—wearing a crewcut and moon-shaped glasses, wobbles out of the bean pit and plops down on the top stair. He looks pale. He clutches his stomach and crooks his head forward. Another man comes up. "Feel all right?" he asks. "A little dizzy," the first man says. He has a thick sheaf of orders bulging out of his smock pocket. "I'll be all right," he says. "Just need a break. I can go back in." The frenzy of trading continues behind him.

After a scattering of good and bad trades that pretty much cancel one another out, Stone emerges with a beaten-down expression on his face. "There are times when you should never have opened your mouth," he says puckishly. "You're trying to force issues. Make things happen. There's nothing there. It's suicide. Sometimes I wish I had masking tape that I could put over my mouth." Interested in strategy, I ask him if there are ways to sucker other traders into bad trades. "Oh, yeah," he says. "Say a guy thinks the market is going to rally. He bids for some beans and nobody sells. He may then bid for a lot more than he really wants, knowing he can't get it, hoping this will indicate a lot of buying interest and will cause the market to rally. But if there's a broker in that pit who has the beans, you'll see that guy turn white awfully fast. There was a case of one guy who would always bid for a big number just to get me to bid up. One day he did it and I wheeled around and said 'Sold' and I thought he was going to croak. I didn't care what it cost me. He immediately offered them back."

"Could he have just said he made a mistake?"

"No way," Stone says. "The minute you open your mouth

in here, that's considered a contract. That's a binding contract. That's why I need masking tape."

I wonder if seasoned traders take advantage of rookies.

"Not the first couple of days," Stone says. "We would help out. After a week, though, he's on his own. Then he's fair game. We're not running a training school here. This is our living. I'm not going to feel sorry for a guy after a week."

Stone wears an attractive, many-carat gold bracelet on the wrist of his left hand. Its presence is dictated not chiefly by aesthetics. It's Stone's lucky piece. His wife gave it to him a few years ago, and he has come to believe that if his left wrist were naked of gold he would make trades that would drain his account. Like all gamblers, traders look for omens and good-luck charms. I heard about individuals who would drive to and from work only along prescribed routes. Whenever they had strayed onto alternate paths, their trading instincts allegedly deserted them in the pits. Other traders would only enter the Board of Trade building through a certain door. Another individual refuses to park his Mercedes in the board's garage as a way to exorcise evil spirits. Still another, a heavy smoker, avoids using a lighter; only matches will do. One trader told me that if he goes home with a position, he makes sure he has an even number of contracts; if he has an odd number, he knows he'll get creamed the next day. There are any number of lucky jackets, lucky shoes patched up beyond the point when most footwear would have been given a respectful burial, lucky ties, lucky handkerchiefs, lucky socks. I heard about a man who has worn the same tie every day since 1963; most of its cloth has disintegrated. A Treasury note trader thinks all socks, whatever their color, are unlucky, so he never wears any. Trading jackets, as a rule, are worn for a week, then returned to the clearinghouse that provided them, to be dry-cleaned. When a trader decides that his jacket has acquired magic that has inspired a streak of winning trades, he forgoes turning it in and takes it home to wash it himself. Why should someone else reap its powers? I have heard of traders who routinely drop quarters into the tins of one of the beggars who patrol the neighborhood, feeling that their generosity will be rewarded in the pit. Traders believe in lucky trading cards. They believe in lucky combs. One man will record his trades only with a purple magic marker. I came across several individuals whose faith in the good luck their pencils brought them was evidenced by the inch-long stubs they used. It seems wiser to rely on a lucky pen.

Commodity traders themselves disagree over whether there is much value in what they do. Many states actually barred futures exchanges at one time, because they deemed them nothing more than casinos. In 1867, the Illinois legislature rose up in wrath and passed a measure to the effect that anyone involved in a futures contract would be fined a thousand dollars and remanded to the Cook County Jail for up to a year. Seven Board of Trade members were in fact arrested under the law before it was repealed the following year. In the Congress, more than a hundred bills designed to banish futures trading have been introduced, though none has gotten terribly far along in the legislative process before being scuttled. In past decades, until the markets got so big and until limits were clamped on how many contracts a trader could hold, some notable plungers managed to manipulate the markets for their own gain. At the turn of the century, a man named Joseph Leiter almost cornered the wheat market, but eventually was driven out of business by Philip Armour, a famous bear. In the late 1920s, Arthur Cutten savaged Jesse Livermore with a forty-million-bushel hurricane of selling. The Hunt brothers of Dallas showed, in their recent ill-fated run on silver, that really big money can still come close to cornering a futures market.

"A lot of people think the exchange is a forum for the locals to make money," Stone tells me one day when we are discussing the economic role of a trader. "It provides an economic function. It provides price discovery for the world. Without the exchanges, you wouldn't know what soybeans are worth. The main economic purpose of the marketplace is to allow an opportunity for a producer to hedge for the future. The prices you see are not set or determined by us. We reflect, like a thermometer, what the supply and demand are. That final price you see up on the board is representative of what the entire world feels that commodity is worth at that time and place."

That may be, but what rankles critics is the fact that many farmers and ranchers are scared silly of the futures markets and never do hedge on them. At the same time, many other classic hedgers (including the Arkansas farmer and the little bakery), seeing the profit opportunities that can be made, are speculating themselves. Nothing wrong with that, as far as the consumer is concerned, when they're right. But when they're wrong, as they often are, then bread is costing more because the bakery felt like throwing the dice, too. The whole debate intensified when stock-index futures were introduced in 1982, enabling an investor to wager on the collective fortunes of the stock market. They were at once branded as thinly disguised betting devices that belonged next to the roulette wheels and one-armed bandits, since, unlike other futures contracts, they weren't backed by anything of intrinsic worth and didn't involve actual delivery of any commodity.

"What we do absolutely isn't gambling," Stone insists. "When I walk in here I can calculate how much risk I want on any trade. My odds are fifty-fifty. The market is either going to go up or go down."

The drinks at the Sign of the Trader are refreshing and bracing, and their price stays steady hour after hour. The place promotes itself as the "third institution" in the Board of Trade building, after the board itself and the Chicago Board Options Exchange. Its bar claims to do the biggest volume of any in the Midwest, and its success is no doubt based on the sound belief that whether a trader has done exceptionally well or poorly, he has good reason to knock back a few. The bar is long and dimly lit. Above it is a green monitor that beams prices and market news. On the menu are such novel delights as the Buyers Salad Bowl, the Sellers Special, and the Board of Trade Favorite (Cheddar cheese, tomato slices, and grilled bacon, toasted under the broiler). A hum of war stories bounces off the walls.

I'm having some liquid refreshment with a trader, not long after the day's close. He asks that I refer to him only as Roger. An ex-stockbroker, he now trades for himself and also operates a clearing firm with a partner. In running a clearinghouse, he is acutely interested in how his traders perform: if they can't cover their losses, Roger and his partner have to scare up the money. He tells me that he instructs new traders to do two things: cut their losses and don't overtrade. He says he has thought of designing a glove to give to novices that would be in the form of a mitten with a single piece of wood protruding upright from it so that, no matter what his inclinations, all the rookie can do is signal for one contract at a time. "No way a man overtrades with a glove like that on," Roger says, chuckling. He informs me that he clears about forty traders, and he's only had two go bust on him. "One guy had a throat operation in which, if the surgeon had slipped, the fellow would have lost his voice. The surgeon didn't slip, but the guy worried a lot about that and he came out a little screwed up in the head. He had a real death wish. He was a consistent loser for a period of time. He came here every day expecting to lose money, and he did. Finally, he sold his seat. I tell you, if you're looking to lose money, there're plenty of guys down here who will oblige you. The other person I told to get out because he was going bad. He just wasn't learning. He wouldn't take his losses. The way I look at it, I'd rather shut somebody off than see him give up his last buck."

Roger got immersed in commodities about eight and a half years ago. His partner in his brokerage house got fed up with the business one day and headed for the floor. Six months later, Roger was cajoled to follow him (and soon after that, Roger persuaded his brother to switch careers, too). He paid forty grand for his seat, which left him with a miserly stake of just two hundred dollars. "I stood next to a guy, and he told me when to buy and when to sell, and I made a few bucks. Things picked up from there." By nature, Roger is circumspect, and even after all his seasoning, he remains a small trader. "Psychologically, it hurts me to go home with a loss. I look at this as a basketball game or a football game. When you start off the day, your adrenaline is running really high, and so it's rough when the day ends to be a loser. I come from Indiana, and my father worked in a steel mill all his life. To this day, it hurts me to lose money. I'll do my damnedest not to lose. I don't mind if I tie. My philosophy is, I just want to be worth a little more than I was the day before." When Roger enjoys a big session in the pits, scoring for a few grand or so, he says he likes to go home and stick crisp new fifty- and hundred-dollar bills on his refrigerator door under magnets, and then tell his wife to go into the kitchen and buy herself some nice things with any money she finds there.

Stone is taking care of some outtrades when I catch up with him on another brisk and icy morning. When a trade made the previous day doesn't square, a so-called outtrade clerk pays a visit the next morning to the traders involved, to give them the deflating news. They then have to settle things before trading commences. I feel a touch sorry for the outtrade clerk, since, to the traders, he represents a form of walking famine. Nobody is ever glad to see him. For all the hastiness of trading, errors are fairly infrequent for a veteran. Most outtrades that occur boil down to nothing more than a slip of the pencil, easily rectified without anyone's reaching for his wallet. On occasion, though, ghastly blunders are committed. "We had an error a month ago in the Treasury bonds where the broker and trader both thought they were buyers," Stone tells me. "There were a hundred contracts involved. That mistake cost each of those gentlemen about two hundred thousand dollars. Not a great way to start the day." When it gets to that kind of money, traders don't come quickly to agreement as to who's at fault, and often the case is taken to a board arbitration committee for refereeing.

Because they never know when a ruinous day may descend on them, traders tend to invest their spare dollars in liquid investments that can be tapped quickly. Treasury bills and money-market funds are popular. If they strike it rich, traders get into oil and real estate and even into sports franchises. Three Chicago traders are the major owners of the Chicago White Sox, and a single trader owns the local soccer team. "If they have extra cash, one thing traders like to have is a smaller mortgage," Stone says, "because if they go bad they don't want to lose their house. If you get into debt, the first thing you lose is your seat. Then it's your house. I know a couple of guys who lost both." Stone has his extra cash stuffed into T-bills and a money fund, and he is looking forward to the day when the mortgage on his condominium shrinks.

"How did you make out yesterday?" I ask him.

"Horrendous," he says dolefully. "I just traded badly. I didn't anticipate the market."

"You lose a few thousand?"

"More than a few thousand."

"How do you feel?"

"Like a horse's ass, if you really want to know."

Trading starts. The noise crescendoes. Stone is on tiptoe more than he is on flat feet, his arms raised so often that one fears for his shoulder joints. After a half-hour, he comes over and reports, "I bought some beans at nine, then somebody behind me bid nine and a half, and so I let him have the beans I just bought. That's a way to make a quick two hundred and fifty dollars." Grinning, he scoots back into the pit.

Behind the bean pit, so-called machine men, traders who gear their actions directly to whatever news chatters over the wire services, are slumped over the Reuters ticker, picking up the latest dope. How's the soybean crush supply? How are Kansas City corn shipments? What were the Winnipeg grain openings?

The din continues:

"I'll sell three and a half. I'll sell three and a half."

"All right, three and a quarter."

"Sell at an eighth. Sell at an eighth."

"Five for an eighth. Five for an eighth. Damnit, give me five for an eighth."

Stone emerges and says, "Jesus, there's one big sell-off going on in there. Every which way you look, somebody's holding up fingers."

Over a late lunch, Stone tells me that the public probably shouldn't fool around with futures. He imparts this advice even though professional traders derive a good chunk of their profits from dull-witted trading by Mr. Average Investor. To the professional, members of the public are looked on as lambs available for fleecing. I recall a conversation I had, after trading one day, with a trader who was grumbling about how unrewarding the session had been because of the dearth of amateur action. "Basically, you have three groups in there," he said. "There are the hedgers, the big grain companies and whatnot, which are sophisticated; the outside professional commodity fund managers, who buy and sell by charts and are sophisticated; and us, who are pit traders and supposedly sophisticated. The public is not in there now, because of high interest rates—they don't have the bucks to gamble, and they can get high returns at no risk. So you've got pros hacking away at other pros to make money. It's very hard. You know, we like to play football games when it's the New York Giants versus the Pelham Blues. We don't like to play when it's the New York Giants versus the Atlanta Falcons."

Nonetheless, I have found that most traders admit that the public is stupid to monkey with futures. Discussing this, Stone tells me that the public is usually unaware of the perils involved. They froth with enthusiasm over the potential riches to be gained, but they close their eyes to the dark side. "I think it's every American's free right to speculate," he says between bites of chicken. "I think when the public speculates they should realize that eighty to ninety percent of the public loses money. They shouldn't speculate with money they need to pay the mortgage. I think all too many of them come into it on a buddy's recommendation—'Hey, I made money in plywood!' They come in and they don't know what the hell they're doing. It's like meat going through a grinder."

The halls are emptying, the trading day is over, the cleaning brigade is on its way to sweep up the oceans of paper, treating winning and losing orders with the same insouciance. Skittering traders are fleeing the floor in long-legged strides. Some are still aburst with energy, others drained. The place is like a funeral parlor compared with the morning din.

Stone is waiting near the exit to meet someone, and I wait with him. Some fellow bean traders shuffle by. As they pass, Stone quizzes them: "How'd you do?" His tone is hushed, as if he were the commanding officer asking the squadron leader just returned from a raid how many fatalities occurred. Some exhibit blank stares; others offer vague responses, such as "It beats running a deli," or "I made a few bucks." (A few bucks, in trader lingo, can mean anything from a few bucks to a few hundred thousand dollars.) More traders go by, filled orders sticking to the soles of their shoes. "It was an okay week for me," Stone says. "I took some bucks out. I enjoy this enough to do it the rest of my life, but I doubt I'll have the stamina. I'd like to keep it up for another ten years or so, then maybe switch to teaching. I like the hours here. I like the people. It's like a fraternity house. I guess it's like *Animal House.*" He glances at the empty bean pit. "Every day that I put on my trading jacket and go in there, I have no idea what's going to happen. I've been petrified some days in that pit. I've also been exhilarated. You get to dream in that pit. Every day, for four hours, you get to dream."

═══FOUR═══

At the Chicago Mercantile Exchange, no view of the outside world distracts traders from their excited questing for money: the trading floor is without windows. Winking price boards blanket three entire walls, and the glassed-in visitors' gallery, through which a steady stream of the curious gaze entranced eight hours a day, takes up the fourth. The floor itself is covered with a nonskid German tile, which I presume cuts the risk of the careening traders' twisting ankles and busting legs. The Mercantile Exchange, which accounts for a quarter of all futures activity and ranks second only to the Board of Trade in volume of contracts, huddles in a modern building on West Jackson Boulevard about a half-dozen blocks from the board, though when you stroll from one exchange to the other during a conventional Chicago winter, the distance seems more like several miles. While I am visiting in Chicago, I decide to turn up my coat collar and trundle over to the Merc to chat with some of its pit traders.

In the second-floor trading room, I wander amid the vibrant noise of contracts changing hands. The faces of the traders and brokers who buzz like bees around the floor are discernibly younger than at the Board of Trade, and the velocity of trading in some of the pits seems just a mite more tenacious, if that's possible. It helps to be young and in fit condition, because the trading hours are longer than those at the board. The Merc, as it happens, is almost as ancient as its bigger brother, and evolved from the Chicago Butter and Egg Exchange, founded in 1898, which at first was nothing more than a convenient place to buy and sell eggs and butter. Then refrigeration enabled farmers to store eggs during the heavy spring supply period for sale in the drowsier fall and winter periods. Thus time contracts came into being. In the 1900s, with the name now changed to the Chicago Mercantile Exchange, contracts in potatoes, onions, and hides were initiated, to be followed by turkeys and frozen eggs. In 1961, the frozen pork belly arrived, which was to develop into one of the most actively traded commodities in the world. Live cattle, the first successful futures contract in a live, nonstorable commodity, was introduced in 1962. It hit it off, and so live hogs and feeder cattle moved in. Nowadays, the Mercantile Exchange controls two divisions: the International Monetary Market and the American Mercantile Market. On the Chicago Mercantile Exchange are traded live cattle, feeder cattle, frozen pork bellies, live hogs, boneless beef, and frozen skinned hams. The AMM trades shell, nestrun, and frozen eggs, lumber, stud lumber, russet Burbank potatoes, frozen turkeys, milo, and butter. The hottest division is the IMM, opened in 1972, which offers financial futures, including seven foreign currencies, U.S. silver coins, and Treasury bills and bonds. In membership makeup, the Board of Trade long was dominated by Protestants and later by Irish Catholics; only recently have Jews infiltrated its pits in any number. The opposite has been the case at the Merc. Jews have always been its principal members, though Protestants and Catholics have been trickling in.

I tail Bill Henner for a few hours while he trades the British pound. He's in his late twenties, with floppy brown hair and a soft voice that I might have thought would spell doom for a pit trader. The pound rarely draws more than a few dozen traders, however, and so vocal projection is of lesser importance than it is in some of the wilder pits. As Henner tells it, he never wanted to become a trader, but, try as he did to follow a different career path, it was probably inevitable that he would wind up screaming for a living, albeit softly. He is a third-generation trader. In essence, his father, also a trader, shanghaied him into the business, and his grandfather traded butter and eggs on the Merc back when butter and eggs were the Merc's bread and butter. Changes in production and marketing, however, have all but killed the contracts. Nowadays, butter is traded just once a week, at 10:00 A.M. on Friday. An exchange official barks, "Any butter contracts, any butter contracts, any butter contracts." If nobody's interested, that's it. Usually nobody bites. Eggs are a little more active, but not much. Henner's father has traded meats on the Merc for some twenty years. "The meats used to be the backbone of the Merc," Henner says. "Now financial futures do double the volume of the meats. There's a limit on how many contracts you can hold in meats. This is to avoid corners and wild fluctuations caused by some big traders. There's no limit in financials. It's pretty impossible to have a corner. I mean, if you want to try to corner the T-bill market, the government will be happy to sell you all you want. If you want to try to corner Swiss francs, the government will be pleased to print up all you want."

Henner went to Stanford and spent about eight years in

the Bay area, sniffing about for his fortune. He sold radio advertising. He sold life insurance. He sold real estate. "My father at first always tried to discourage me from the business. He wanted me to be a doctor. He thought there were philosophically better things for me to do. This business doesn't really provide great benefit for people." But Henner got bored in California, and his father, a big trader who had enjoyed fabulous success, was looking to take more time off and wanted someone he could trust to mind his positions while he floated on his yacht. "My father figured that if I was going to stay in selling, I might as well come down here, where it's more interesting and potentially more lucrative." Finally, in September 1978, Henner left the sunshine and entered the pits. He had worked one summer as a runner when he was seventeen, which gave him a rudimentary knowledge of the floor. He picked up the rest by immersing himself in books explaining the intricacies of the markets. He then deepened his comprehension by moving onto the floor itself. "I started small. It was difficult. It's still difficult."

The British pound trades in a fairly compact pit arranged against the far wall. Next to it are similarly sized pits for the Japanese yen, the Swiss franc, and the deutsche mark, all of which are somewhat interrelated in their trading behavior. "The language is a little different here from at the Board of Trade," Henner tells me. "There they say 'Sold' when something's bought. Here they say 'Buy it.'"

Henner is very technically oriented. He gets to his office in the Board of Trade building at 6:30 A.M., rubs his eyes, and peruses his charts, then hustles over to the Merc to catch the pound opening at 7:35. "There are fewer and fewer guys who follow fundamentals," he says. "They believe they're represented in the charts. The problem is, you can be absolutely fundamentally right and things may be going the way you expect in the long run, but the market may go differently for technical reasons in the short run and you can get blown out of the market and lose a lot of money."

Henner does some position trading when he feels comfortable with his charts, but the market has been so unpredictable lately that he has concentrated on scalping.

Henner races in and out of the ring. When he comes out and talks, one eye is always glued to the big electronic price board. When he spots something he likes, he politely excuses himself and darts into the pit. He comes out at 8:51. He furrows his brow and a bewildered expression plays across his face. "I went in there and lost five hundred dollars right away," he says in a chipper tone. "Then I came back. I'm up about a hundred dollars right now."

Things quickly settle down. Henner emerges and says, "It's like pulling teeth in there today. There's no volume." Two brokers in the pit find the time to place bets on the weekend pro football matchups. They have a conflict on the Denver game: both want Denver. A purple-faced trader comes out of the pit yelling, "I want a Milk Dud. I want a Milk Dud." A broker, surprisingly enough, hands him a Milk Dud. Someone shuffles by from the Swiss franc pit. His tie boasts a painting of himself yanking clumps of dollar bills out of his jacket pockets and thrusting them wildly into the air. I spot a runner with a button: "We will sell no swine before its time." Somebody wobbles by and declares to no one in particular, "I get so high on this floor that it's like doing cocaine. I just want to play this game."

As a matter of fact, quite a few traders have been said not only to like to play the game but to do cocaine, too. An active drug trade, much of it dealt by runners, has flourished for some time on the floor. Things cooled off somewhat when, in

1979, Drug Enforcement Administration agents showed up on the floor of the Chicago Board Options Exchange and carted away ten individuals, three of them besmocked traders, stuffing them into paddy wagons and charging them with possession and trafficking of the white stuff. Nevertheless, some of the young clerks told me that there was still plenty of cocaine to be had for those who could afford it.

One trader, presumably averse to wasting time, is doing the Chicago *Tribune* crossword puzzle on the fringe of the pound pit. In goes a word. He hears an offer he likes. In goes a bid. In goes another word. Gray hair. Glasses. Maybe forty-five. He walks forward. Fifteen for four Deece. In goes a word. Argali.

The snack bar adjacent to the floor entrance is equipped with shiny machines that dispense cellophane-wrapped sandwiches, potato chips, pretzels, and a miscellany of beverages. A trader can buy his lunch off these walls. Many do, slouching into the automatic-vending-machine room and depositing their dimes and quarters, giving more thought to whether to go for the tuna sandwich or a corned beef than they seemed to give to betting thousands on March hogs rather than April pigs. I go over and buy a can of root beer. Sucking the soda through a straw, I catch fragments of conversation among the traders similarly occupied.

"The markets are just heartless today. I'm trading well. I mean, really well. And I'm getting my head handed to me."

"I've got a suggestion."

"What's that?"

"Stay in here and eat sandwiches. It's a lot cheaper. Just keep going long sandwiches."

"For a few moments there, I thought I had a golden voice. Everything I took shot right up."

"Then what happened?"

"I resumed my usual crappy trading."

"How're bonds?"

"So-so."

"How're marks?"

"Absolute puke."

"Well, you've always traded puke with great insight and verve."

On the other side of the entryway is a members' lounge, a cluster of ordinary-looking chairs and couches that have seen far better days and some end tables piled with popular magazines, which provides a temporary and blissful sanctuary from the phantasmagoria of the floor. I have noticed that throughout the day—with the obvious exception of the first hour of trading, when everyone is crammed into the pits— the lounge generally is thick with exhausted traders, blank looks on their faces, their brains seemingly perforated, mustering the energy to get back into the battle. Some of the traders arranged there now seem a bit at loose ends. One man is fast asleep and snoring. Another one is reading a moldy paperback thriller. Someone else seems on the verge of tears. A young woman, in fact, *is* in tears. "You've got to take breaks here," a thick-featured trader lolling against the wall informs me. "You can't hang out in those pits every minute they're open. It's brutal. You'd be ready for a casket. So you come in here and bullshit. Sometimes you come in here and just faint. I'm contemplating fainting right now."

While I'm peering at some monitors flashing the latest business news, Michael Rockin comes up to me. His game is the Swiss franc. Rockin tells me that he is not yet a full-fledged Mercantile member: he leases his seat from a retired trader who has repaired to balmier climates. He informs me that his current seat rent is $2,800 a month; when he began two years ago, the rate was $1,500. There is no such thing as rent control in trading seats.

In elaborating on his debut on the floor, Rockin tells me that he had been working for a trader named Morris at Morris's clearinghouse ("My position was peasant"), when he became ensnarled in some sort of romantic triangle or quadrangle that, when he explains it to me, seems more complicated than even the more convoluted episodes of "As the World Turns." The bottom line was that Rockin had to be axed. Morris, though, wasn't all that miffed at him, and as consolation he backed Rockin so he could lease a seat and go trade on the floor. Rockin likes to say, when asked how he got into the business, "I was fired and was given a seat as severance."

Rockin has a short mustache, thick glasses, thinning hair, and a birthmark covering one side of his face. His pint size means that he must stand in the very middle of the Swiss pit to get an adequate perspective on what is being offered. He is very much wedded to the idea of talking, and I imagine that if he were in the Swiss pit during a lull, when nobody was making any trades, Rockin would pipe up and take some francs just to have something to say. He is thirty-five and often laments the fact that he did not discover trading the day he accepted his college diploma. First he picked up a CPA and practiced accounting for a couple of years, which was all it took for him to tire of columns of numbers. Then he embarked on six years of playing the horses for a living. His luck ran out in time, and he took a job managing what he describes as "a high-class pizza joint." That career was quickly scotched when Rockin was fired. He decided his prime options were "used cars, insurance, or a runner's job."

After some debate, he took the runner's position with Morris's clearinghouse, and it has been bliss ever since.

Rockin likens trading, in certain key respects, to betting on the horses, though he finds it far more reliable. "It's easier here," he tells me over the babble of voices, "because there are only two horses: the market can only go up or go down. And you can call off the race any time you want."

The floor has had other appeals for him lacking in a lifetime presiding over the preparation of pasta. "If you're wrong here, you can't blame the weather," he says cheerfully. "You can't blame the moon. You have to look in the mirror and say, Okay, buddy-boy, it's me." During his early sprees in the pits, Rockin barely scraped by ("No one wins at the beginning; people who never admit to losing admit to losing at the beginning"), though his fortunes have since begun looking upward. "Now, I'm self-supporting. I've made more money here than I ever thought I could make. I made six figures this year, and I have no complaints. I made eleven hundred dollars today." When I ask him his technique, he replies, "I read headlines in the paper, *TV Guide*, *Time*, and *Sports Illustrated*. I also do my own charts. That takes about ten minutes. Also, I usually assume the opposite position from everyone else's. It's more fun."

To have still more fun, Rockin subscribes to a number of unprovable and certainly unorthodox theories. He believes that the Swiss never has a range of more than 115 points. He feels pretty sure that the Swiss enjoys its biggest downside potential on days when it opens highest. He insists that it is important, when he goes home with an active position, that he own an even number of contracts. To be sure, Rockin will not stake much more than perhaps a soft drink on the certainty of such theories: "There are no 'never's here. This is a pure social science. There are lots of 'frequently's, 'rarely's, 'often's."

He takes a few notes on some of the news appearing on the monitors, his head bobbing up and down and his hand moving at just about the speed of light; then he returns to our conversation. "In normal street terms, if you make a hundred thousand dollars, that's a very big living. Here, if you make a hundred thousand dollars, that's an okay living. You don't have to work hard, but you're no star."

Which is not to say that, on his way to becoming something short of a star, Rockin has not had his apportionment of dark days. A couple of months ago, he watched forty thousand dollars atrophy from his account during two days of misdirected trading. His medicine for adversity in the pits is to run many miles across open fields. He believes he may have huffed over thirty miles the weekend following the tumult of those two days.

His opinion is that, if a moderate living is all that one needs, then trading can be a fairly comfortable profession. From his observations, most traders—80 percent or more— make it at the calling. "The only way you wouldn't make it is to be an idiot. You have to be a masochist. You have to like the pain of losing. The big winners are sadists. You couldn't go on the street and take a hundred people and bring them here and have most of them make it. But if you find a hundred sadists, most would. Sadism is the key."

"You truly believe that?" I say.

"Yeah, being a sadist is really important," Rockin replies. "You have to really want to stick it to people. Somebody on the floor wears a button that says 'I don't get mad, I get even.' That's a pretty sadistic remark, in my book."

I ask him what drew him to the Swiss franc.

"I tried every pit on the floor. You wander aimlessly through the maze until you find something you like. I tried the British pound. I tried spreading the gold. I tried the deutsche mark. Then I tried the Swiss pit and I liked it. Each pit has its own personality."

"What's the personality of the Swiss franc pit?"

"Basically vermin. We will cut each other's throat. Some guys won't set foot in the Swiss pit. In the Swiss, everyone's an enemy. I just love the days when you can smell blood. When you're the only person who's right, it's great fun."

"Is trading gambling?" I ask.

"Isn't everything gambling?" he says crisply. "If you walk across the street, you could get hit by a car. Isn't everything a game? It's no different than selling a tuna-fish sandwich. You take some tuna out of the can and put some mayonnaise on it and you put some salt and pepper on it and you slap on some bread and you try to make it for a dollar and sell it for a dollar-fifty. You're serving a purpose by selling that tuna-fish sandwich, but you're in it for the money. We're all whores. The thing is, a commodity trader is more apt to admit he's a whore than a doctor or a lawyer is."

"That doesn't bother you."

"I'm a whore and I admit it. I suppose that makes me better than some others."

"What if floor traders were outlawed?"

"The world wouldn't stop turning, that's for sure," Rockin says. "The world would still go around every twenty-four hours."

Rockin is getting a little edgy about being absent from the Swiss franc pit and its pack of sadists for such a spell, and so he heads back after leaving me with a final reflection: "There are very few independent floor traders. Most guys do some brokerage work. They do work for banks. The best thing is to be an independent trader. You know why? There's no ass to kiss. You do something else, you have to be nice to your boss. You have to tell him his wife is pretty. You have to tell him you like his pipe tobacco. Here, you don't have to be anything or do anything. You just have to be good. Me, I try very hard to be an asshole, and most people seem to agree I accomplish my goal. It doesn't matter. Nobody can touch me. I don't have to kiss any ass."

Burt Costello is solid and bewhiskered. The whiskers are white. Costello looks like a lumberjack, a Santa Claus out of costume, a bit player from "The Waltons." He has on a raddled sweater. He is straddling a chair in the office of the Sinclair Brokerage Corporation, his clearinghouse, up on the thirtieth floor of the Mercantile building. There is a large wooden desk in the office, on which rest two bottles of sore-throat spray, a trader's best friend. Two additional desks have been shoved against the far wall without regard for aesthetics; atop them sit four Zenith television sets. On the screens, traveling via closed-circuit wires, are the price boards of the various commodities traded downstairs. I can imagine few less interesting television programs to watch, with the possible exception of the always burning Yule log that gets broadcast each Christmas Eve. For a professional trader, though, price boards lead the Nielsen ratings. The TV hookups allow traders worn out by the skirmishing down on the floor to recharge themselves without losing track of what's happening in the pits. If something looks good, there are phones available on the desk.

Costello, who trades currency and cattle, is sitting and watching the hermetic silence of the TVs rather than standing and bellowing in the pits because he has been temporarily grounded. He was unable to reconcile a sizable outtrade with another trader, and his clearinghouse did not support him. Oh, screw this—Costello more or less said—I'll fight it. While his case wheezes toward arbitration, he has taken up with Sinclair, though bureaucratic procedures take several days before he can be shipped back to the pits. "I feel like a caged man up here," Costello says.

Costello grew up in Wilmington, Illinois, where $10,000 a year was all he ever hoped to earn. He attended Illinois State with the intention of becoming a schoolteacher. When he was done with his education, the first teaching contract dangled his way amounted to $3,200 a year. It was not the kind of catch he had in mind, and he decided to cast his line in other streams. He drifted into Chicago and fell into sales work. He sold typewriters and finished metal products. In time, he rose to manager of a Japanese trading company. One day he met a well-to-do commodities trader who also operated a sales firm. This trader hired Costello as a sales manager. In 1965, the man lent him the money to buy a Mercantile seat, and, as Costello puts it, "I've been on the roller coaster ever since."

His first year on the floor, Costello made two thousand dollars trading pork bellies, and schoolteaching no longer looked so bad. For a while, he mostly filled orders, but in the fall of 1971, he started trading for himself as well. He had good years up through 1975; then he had to sell his membership as a means of self-preservation. He had guaranteed a loan to two friends (pledging his membership for the loan), and both he and they were going bad; since he was afraid of losing his seat, he sold it. From 1977 through the first half of 1979, he traded soybeans at the Board of Trade. In 1979, he lost about four hundred thousand dollars in four days, and quit. "That was a perfectly good sign that the Board of Trade didn't like me too much. I was long beans in a bull market. It's called dumb." He holed up at home and traded from there for a while, before returning to the Merc.

"The biggest trade I ever made was I made forty-seven thousand dollars once on an opening," Costello says. "It was a pork-belly trade in, let's see, 1973. I sold some contracts on the opening and a minute later had a forty-seven-thousand-dollar profit. It's nothing to brag about. I know guys who in a day of day trading have made four hundred thousand dollars. Now, *that's* good money."

I remark that lots of traders seem to have difficulty hanging on to their bonanzas for very long.

"All of us are just sort of living on borrowed money," Costello says. "We borrow some bucks from that market there, then she asks for it back. She's a fickle lady. Quite a few guys like to go to Vegas on the weekends for some fun. Now, Vegas can really empty your pockets fast. On the other hand, there's a kid on the floor who lost two hundred thousand dollars on Monday and Tuesday. On Friday, he was playing baccarat in Reno and made two hundred and fifty thousand. That's very unusual. It's generally the other way around: you make it here and blow it there."

Costello snatches up one of the mouth sprays, opens wide, and gives himself a good blast. It seems to act like a jump on a dead battery. He wrinkles his nose and says, "If Saint Peter ever asked me about a commodity trader, whether he was the worst person on earth or the best, the thing to remember is two things. There are two billion people on this earth. There are about five thousand, tops, who make their living just doing commodity trading. No one signs their checks. They have to be winners. They're willing to take risks. Secondly, on any given day, you're trading big money. The week before last, I traded three hundred million worth of commodities per day. Every trade that I made was on the honor system. I trust the guy I traded with to turn in the trade as we did it, and he trusts me to do it. Jews, Irishmen, Poles, Far Easterners, Middle Easterners, every ethnic background, every educational background is out there. There are guys on the floor with MBAs from Harvard and there are guys who have no more than a high-school education. You could shoot a guy down every day, but it rarely happens."

"Are you always so high on the business?" I ask. "Isn't it a drag when you keep losing?"

"I don't know if I've ever been totally depressed," Costello says. "You're pissed off at yourself, you're not depressed. You know you're going to make a winning trade again. You're afraid that you're not going to, but you always, down deep, think you are."

He blows his nose, sounding something like a tugboat warning horn, and goes on: "The worst year is this year. I don't think I've made fifty thousand dollars. People are getting better—the public is getting better—so it's tougher. There are new, young people. The average age when I came down here was probably fifty. Now it's probably thirty. The younger guys got the big edge. We used to trade nine to twelve-thirty. Now you have to get down here at seven and get out at two-thirty to trade financials, where the volume is. You've got to be six-eight and a karate champion to get into the bond pit. The pits are much more crowded.

"It's getting tougher and tougher. The traders are better and better. Everyone's getting better. It's more physical. I used to wear good shoes in the pits. Now I wear work boots. You get stepped on, you get punched, you get pencils stuck in your eyes. Yeah, it's a lot more physical.

"You gotta take breaks now. You gotta take breaks. I would

say the number-one ailment today is alcoholism. The second is hemorrhoids. It's pressure, pressure, pressure. Every time the number changes up there, somebody's happy and somebody's sad. It's constant decision-making. Do I cover, do I take my loss, do I take my profits? This is a character-developing business. It builds character—and there are a lot of characters in the business."

A trader stamps into the Sinclair office, fuming. "I've sucked about fifteen Gs in the Jap yen and I didn't even get a chance to breathe," he says.

"Easy come fifteen Gs, easy go fifteen Gs," hoots another trader, offering about all the consolation the man is going to get.

"I'm going home short four cows," a second arrival declares to the room. "There's nothing I can do. I'll go home short the cows. I just don't believe these cattle."

The man who owes cows is, in fact, an electrician. More precisely, he is a quasi-electrician, since he is also a quasi-trader. His name is Al Thomas. At fifty-two, he has salt-and-pepper hair, aviator glasses, a waistline slightly beyond the borders of prime marketability. Thomas owns a six-million-dollar electrical-contracting business. Friends lured him into trading. When he first experienced the floor, he saw nothing there for him. "I used to come down here and I thought these guys were crazy." Sinking into craziness, he took a course in charting, purchased a microcomputer, and decided to hit the floor. "I've been down here two years now and I'm still learning. I've not yet gotten hurt, but I haven't made any money yet. I spent four years as an apprentice as an electrician, so I'm in no rush."

"Why the move from putting in electricity to pulling out money?"

"I've been involved all my life in unions, insurance companies, customers, receivables, payrolls. None of that is down here. Here, if you're wrong, you're wrong. If you're right, you feel like a hero."

Thomas is by nature an early riser. He bounds down to the Mercantile Exchange in the breakfast hours and trades currencies and live cattle, then takes off at lunchtime to tend to his electrical errands. At night, he puts together his charts.

"I lost eight hundred dollars this morning before I even walked onto the floor. But then I went down there and made sixteen hundred dollars on cattle. You gotta clear your head. You've got to have the guts to slug it out. Some guys, when they take a loss, they just collapse. Emotionally, they can't do it. I was that way when I came down here."

"The key," Costello interrupts, as he leaves the room to take a phone call in privacy, "is you don't make it as easy as you lose it."

"I never enter a market unless the odds are three-to-one risk factor," Thomas goes on by way of explaining his particular trading quirks. "I figure that, out of three trades, I'm going to lose on two but make more on that third than the two losses."

Costello lumbers back into the room. I ask him why he trades. "I'm addicted to it," he answers. "Where else can I have the opportunity to make big bucks? I'm accustomed to a high life-style." He lives in a big old farmhouse set on four acres. He has a couple of cars, a couple of dogs.

A lot of years in the pits tends to instill in professionals a somewhat overblown concept of the delights of their calling. The rest of the world begins to seem routine, if not downright boring. "You're really living life to its fullest down here," Costello continues. "Say a guy works nine to five and makes fifty thousand dollars a year. Maybe the biggest decision he makes during the day is whether he should cross the street against the red or not. He knows he's got a check at the end of the week. He knows he's got a wife at home who will put a meal on the table. Here you've got to make a million decisions. Those pits are a mirror of life. All the ups and downs of life go on in those pits."

In trading routine, Costello is neither a chartist nor a fundamentalist. He depends on a mathematical system that he is emphatically secretive about. He bought it some years ago from someone he describes as a "self-taught mathematical genius." It cost him a hundred thousand dollars. Seven individuals own it, including a lawyer, a stock broker, and a chicken farmer. If someone were willing to put up a quarter of a million dollars for the system today, he or she couldn't get one: the seven buyers made a pact that only a restricted number of people would have access to it. For a hundred thousand dollars, Costello received a single sheet of paper explaining the technique. "It takes fifteen minutes a day to bring it up to date. It's right four out of five times. It tells you when a market is going to turn and gives you the price at which a given market is going to turn."

I ask Costello, "With such a terrific system, why have you been having such a disappointing year?"

He grins and says, "I let the art override the science."

Costello hoists himself up and sidles over to me and taps my right knee. "If you decided to make a trade when your right foot is crossed over your left foot, and you make it every time that left foot is over the right, you're going to make money. Because it's a discipline. If one time you don't follow that rule, you'll lose it all."

He stuffs himself back into his seat. Then he raises a point, by now familiar to me, about accepting losses. "The hardest thing in the world is to learn how to lose. You're winner-oriented. Just like we're buyer-oriented. Why is the public always long? You don't go to the retail store to sell a suit. Buying is almost primordial. There are damned few guys down here who are successful. That's because there are damned few of us who know how to lose."

I ask Costello what happens to the guys who tip out.

He nibbles at his nails and says, "There's one guy who, the first time he went busted, went out and drove a cab until he made enough money to come back on the floor. Now he's one of the richest guys on the floor. He had a Kentucky Derby winner. We were talking before about a guy who bought his membership the same year I did. He wasn't a good trader. He had five opportunities to make it. He's now driving a truck in Minnesota. He always wanted to be a truck driver. Now he's got it, after being a millionaire several times."

FIVE

Often during a period of some months, I have gotten into the habit of taking trips down to the World Trade Center and spending time watching the trading at the Commodity Exchange Center. On most of my visits there, my guide is a trader named Warren Schwartz. Schwartz is a talkative, hyperactive man just over forty. He has frizzy black hair with flecks of gray, and a mustache that reaches around his mouth. He looks slightly Mephisthophelean, though his manner is cheerful, with a frequent shaft of dry wit. Even during calmer moments, he appears to have just gulped down an urn of black coffee. Even when he is sitting still, he seems to be in motion. He is an adept guide. His enthusiasm is infectious. As he nears the trading floor, he sometimes looks to the sky and lets out a cowboy yell, swiveling his head back just in time to avoid trampling some elderly woman burdened with packages.

I can never be sure what Schwartz will be trading. He always has itchy feet. When I first met him, he would start off in the cocoa ring at the New York Mercantile Exchange, shrieking and fidgeting like a condemned man. About twenty minutes later, he'd whip over to the gasoline ring, where he would resume his bellowing. After a brief fling at gas, he would migrate to the adjacent ring and go hoarse trading heating oil. When things got hotter in one of the other commodities traded on the floor, he would switch his allegiance. I would run into Schwartz after not seeing him for a week or ten days and he would say, "Guess what, I'm trading sugar now." About his fickleness, he often says, "I'll trade anything. I'll trade orange juice, lime juice, prune juice. I'll trade inner tubes. I'll trade sand. I'll trade air. I'll trade Melba toast. I know zilch about these things. But I'll trade them. I look at it this way: if I had to trade chopped liver, I'd trade chopped liver."

A Thursday morning. Early fall. The weather is sharp. Schwartz and I have just finished wolfing down a high-cholesterol breakfast at Harry's Restaurant in the heart of New York's financial district, and are heading for the Mercantile Exchange. Schwartz is looking particularly sportive. He is smartly turned out in an orange-and-white Madras shirt, white cotton slacks, and soft brown loafers without socks. He is jacketless, looking vaguely like a skipper about to embark on a day of yachting. He is already wound up, talking fast and walking fast. I am not certain, but I suspect he is breathing fast.

"Time out," he suddenly says, and with a sense of some urgency, as if he has just remembered that he left the bathtub running four hours ago, he applies the brakes, makes an abrupt left, and scoots over to a candy stand. He studies the confusing selection of cough drops, candies, and gums before picking out a package of breath mints. "They won't trade with you if your breath is bad," he says. "I tell you, you gotta watch your breath on the floor."

The Commodity Exchange Center, the country's third-biggest futures market, is eight floors up the quick-rising elevators of the Southeast Plaza Building of the World Trade Center. Here, the cramped mayhem of four futures exchanges—the New York Mercantile Exchange, the New York Cotton Exchange, the Commodities Exchange, and the Coffee, Sugar and Cocoa Exchange—are bunched together in one antiseptic room. Each exchange, though, requires its own membership. As it happens, Schwartz owns seats on three of the four (he has no seat in cotton) and therefore can try his luck at almost any ring in the room. "It's like a casino," he says. "You walk around and put twenty dollars on this game, put twenty dollars on this game, put twenty dollars on that game." After a tall, severe-looking man issues me a visitor's badge, and a sour-faced security guard brushes a metal detector up and down my briefcase (bomb threats are occasional events here), we are free to enter the trading room. It is already beginning to fill up with people—plowing past with their hands clutching trading cards, their faces grave and determined. A plush maroon carpet snuggles the floor. Clustered around the perimeter are the obligatory booths for phone clerks. The center is reserved for octagonal structures sunk several steps down, with blond wooden railings and glossy steel supports that, despite their shape, are always referred to as "rings" (in Chicago, "pit" is the preferred word)—the cherished holy ground of the traders. As at the Chicago exchanges, pulsing electronic tote boards decorate the walls. Men and women—many of them fairly young and somewhat scruffy, and a good deal of them in extremely casual garb (I even spotted several women in bare feet)—totter to and fro across the cavernous floor. I distinctly hear one middle-aged trader say, with a certain quiver of desperation in his voice, "Lord have mercy, let silver rise today. I will never sin again if only silver rises."

Nonchalantly slouched against the Gulf Coast heating-oil

ring, which is completely dead for the moment, Schwartz pores over his clearing sheets, which inform him in stark black digits, with no hint of congratulation or condolence, of how he made out during yesterday's trading session, most of which he spent hugging the heating-oil ring. This is his daily post-mortem. Today he remarks that he plans to check out cocoa—he's got a modest position there—to see what's happening, but he doesn't expect he'll do any heavy trading. Interest in cocoa has been kind of languid lately. Schwartz's luck has been dismal. Much more is cooking in heating oil. "I think heating oil is going to be the biggest thing around," he says. "Let's face it, the world needs heating oil. You want to get warm, you need heating oil. It's a lubricant. I mean, with cocoa, do you need it? Do you really need it? Cotton? Orange juice? Sure, they're nice to have. Can you live without them? Not heating oil. Heating oil has got to be the most important commodity around."

A chubby man with a vacant, headachy look taps Schwartz on the shoulder and shovels a folded, mimeographed sheet of paper into his hand. I am told that this is "Dock's Charting Data," a document that Schwartz and a number of other traders buy that consists of an agglomeration of predictions for contracts of different commodities. The price is three hundred dollars a month. Compiled by a floor broker named Dock, it points out when a contract will "break down," or skid to a price that will encourage people to start selling in bulk, and when it will "break out," or rocket to an extent that speculators will likely buy heavily to cover short positions. Schwartz doesn't swear by the sheet, relying chiefly on sparks of intuition, but he takes its picks into account when he's trading. "It's like a tip sheet at the track," he says. "Sometimes it works, sometimes it doesn't." Schwartz is basically a spread trader, and a highly skilled one. "Knowing a good spread is just inbred in me," he says. "Not that I'm always right. I had a spread yesterday that collapsed on me like a matzoh."

Returning his gaze to his clearing sheets, Schwartz performs a little mental arithmetic, and happiness beams from his face. He says, "Well, I made three thousand dollars yesterday trading heating oil. A day's pay. It's a game. It's a store. I have no phone. I borrow a pencil. I steal stationery from the exchange. And my dues are two hundred and fifty dollars a year. That's my rent. Where can you buy a business like that in America? Think about it. A grocery store has got to cost you a hundred thousand dollars when you finish putting in the canned peas and the Diet Pepsi and the Wheaties. This has to be the greatest business in America. Where can you know so little and make so much? Look at these hands. What can they do? Dig phone lines? Nah. What am I capable of doing? Think about it."

Schwartz, for reasons he is not altogether sure of, has a predilection to believe that at any moment the sky stands a good chance of collapsing. The apocalypse will arrive. To characterize Schwartz as a cynic is to soft-pedal the word. He revels in dying markets, and tends to celebrate his biggest winnings when prices plummet. "I'm like the undertaker," he is wont to say of himself. "I'm waiting for the bodies to come in. They're going to come in sooner or later, and I'm waiting for them. I got the graves all dug." Another time Schwartz tells me, "I've made a lot of money off of death." Acquaintances on the floor, when they spot Schwartz heading their way, joke, "Hey, here comes Mr. Optimist." Not long ago, a friend, noticing Schwartz, called out, "Hey, Warren, I hear you're happy. Three guys got hit by a truck outside."

Schwartz lives in Cliffside Park, New Jersey, and typically

drives his Mercedes in to work. Often, he gives a neighbor who works in the Wall Street area a lift. One morning, while they were tooling through some dense traffic, Schwartz began his customary diatribe on the woes of the world. They were nowhere near the World Trade Center when it was patently clear from the evidence put forth by Schwartz that your money was safe nowhere. The neighbor was thankful that the ride was costing him nothing, because it seemed that every dime was going to count. The trip got increasingly depressing. When they arrived, as he lifted himself out of the car, the neighbor swung around to look at Schwartz and said, "You know, Warren, after riding with you, I feel like killing myself."

His bleak outlook for the country's prospects have convinced Schwartz to adopt certain precautions to guard against being reduced to utter poverty. He fears that the economy might self-destruct at any moment. He foresees rioting in the streets. He worries that it will be necessary for him to flee the country. Short of having packed his bags, he is all ready to go. He has purchased a hundred and sixty thousand dollars' worth of Swiss francs, which are safely stashed away in a Swiss bank. When the first riots begin, Schwartz expects to get on the next plane to Australia. On arriving there, he will wire for his cache, take it easy, wait until things settle down again. Then and only then will he resume his daily pilgrimages to the futures rings.

One of the things I like best about Schwartz is the fact that he is a habitual truthteller. Many traders, especially when they are talking to the public, are fond of making grand pronouncements about the critical economic niche they fill. When I ask Schwartz for a summary of what good he does jumping around the commodity rings, his reply is: "I provide a little bit of liquidity. Other than that, I serve no economic purpose at all. Zippo. I'm what you call a leech. I'm a high-class bloodsucker."

The opening of the metal palladium greets the ears with a painful burst of noise. Perking up at the clamor, Schwartz suggests that we go over to survey the scene. By now, he knows traders at all of the rings and he likes to see who's making money and who's losing it.

"Personally, I say what I think about people," Schwartz tells me en route to the palladium ring. "Some guys think, well, if they're too blunt, then some other guys won't trade with them. Listen, if I've got something somebody else wants at a price I'm willing to sell at, or if I offer to buy some lots for a price somebody else likes, they'll trade with me. That's all that really matters down here: prices."

Trading sometimes makes for short tempers. Within a few minutes of the opening bell, a bitter argument flares up between two men positioned at opposite ends of the palladium ring. One of the combatants is a dyspeptic-looking but husky bear of a man. His opponent is a stringy fellow who, if forced into physical combat, wouldn't stand a chance against the bigger man if he had Sugar Ray Leonard at his side. None of that seems to enter into his thinking. The two uncork a torrent of abuse.

"What the hell do you think you're doing?" the big man hollers. "Who the fuck do you think you are? That was my trade. Give me that trade, you miserable bastard."

"Get the hell out of here," the stringy provocateur retorts frostily, his voice a few decibels below sonic. "You're crazy. You don't know where you're coming from, you jerk. You're out of your ever-lovin' mind."

"That's my goddamn trade," the first man counters, his

voice having risen *above* sonic level. "Give me that. Cut this crap. That's my goddamn trade."

"Take a fucking leap."

"Up yours."

Meanwhile, the dozen or so traders crammed around the ring stand in amusement, a few of them expressing their own personal preferences with catcalls such as "C'mon, Bill, bust the squirt," or "Ram it down his throat."

"It's always like this," Schwartz tells me calmly. "There are always arguments in palladium. This is why a lot of guys won't trade across the ring. They're afraid of mistakes. They'll only trade with guys next to them."

Finally, apparently having run out of all the barnyard epithets he knows, the first trader sneers, throws up his hands in frustration, and concedes defeat to the second man, though he makes it clear that he is hardly pleased about the outcome. "You're an asshole," he informs his foe. "You're a real piece of scum."

Chortling at this agitation, Schwartz meanders around the floor some more, dispensing greetings to fellow traders.

"Hey kid, how ya doing?"

"Okay, Warren, how're you?"

"Hey, what's happening, kid?" Schwartz says to a frowning cocoa trader. (Traders seem to have a propensity for addressing everyone, regardless of age, as "kid.")

"Not much."

"You still alive?"

"Yeah, I'm alive."

"As long as you're still breathing, kid. As long as you're gulping air."

Clomping past the sugar ring, Schwartz bumps into a trader named Gary, a sharp-faced man in his late thirties with a small abrasion on his chin, who informs him that he's taking a hiatus from the business for a while. He's been down on the floor, bellowing bids, for eight years. When he started trading, his pockets were virtually empty, but things went his way for a long time and he ran up his slender stake to some 3.5 million dollars. In 1980, when the silver market collapsed after the Hunts got a mite too greedy, he dropped 1.5 million, a debacle softened only by the fact that he still had a couple of million left.

"Eight years here, and I never took a day's vacation," he says, shaking his head. "This floor becomes an obsession. I want some time off. I want to get my head together. I want to spend the money. I want to get up and spend eight hundred dollars, a thousand dollars a day. I want to spend the money already."

"So," Schwartz says, "go spend the money."

Nine-thirty. The cocoa ring opens for business. Schwartz lurks on the perimeter of the crowd of traders, curious about price swings but not overly anxious to get mixed up in the action. "I'm getting chopped in cocoa," he says. "Every time I go here, they bust me like I was a felon."

One trader thrusts his arm forward to make a bid and accidentally releases his pencil; it sails across the ring and caroms off the head of a balding man in the third row. The balding man, who is in the process of offering a bid, continues unfazed. Schwartz, over the years, has had three gold bracelets slip off as he waved a bid and fly across one ring or another, lost forever. Now he wears a Cartier bracelet that is so tightly bound to his wrist that two screws must be removed to get it off.

I watch a telephone pole of a man making trades with lightning speed, his face brightening each time he completes another. He seems to have a gleam of wisdom about him, and indeed I am told he has a reputation for having good information and consistently being in the money. Across the way, an apple-cheeked trader who looks barely pubescent is ladling money into the ring, barely finishing one bad trade before he offers another. Traders quickly sense when someone is stinking up the ring, and they react by stripping him of as much of his capital as they can manage. "The answer," Schwartz says to me in explaining why one trader cleans up while another takes daily baths, "is that if you want to make a lot of money you've got to be ten percent better than the next guy. It's like a quarterback. You think the difference between the best and the worst quarterback is so great? Same with traders."

Schwartz hears nothing that greatly piques his interest. His enthusiasm dampened, he wanders off to heating oil.

"To be honest, average guys do well here," Schwartz tells me as we walk. "None of them is particularly smart. You don't have to be smart. The guys who do well here just have values programmed into their heads. Instinct is what you need. It's like knowing your brother."

"We've got four minutes till heating oil," Schwartz says. "Gotta get ready. Gotta warm up. Gotta do some stretching exercises." Whereupon he awkwardly executes, in non–Jack LaLanne fashion, a series of jumping jacks. Some traders stare at Schwartz and smile; others stare at him and give no sign that they see anything out of the ordinary. Schwartz is a strange amalgam. He has a passionate interest in money. Most other things bore him. I have found him, during encounters on the court, to be an interesting tennis player (he hits enough high lobs to bring thunderous rain on cloudless days), but I doubt that he is impassioned about knocking a spherical object back and forth across a net. Schwartz's wife, Enid, is an interior decorator. Their condominium in Cliffside Park is a dazzling showplace of what she can do. It has no effect on Schwartz. Heating-oil drums would look good to him as dining-room chairs. He would sleep in a casket. Talk to him for any length of time about anything other than commodity futures and he changes the conversation back or just looks away. Once I asked Enid what Schwartz appreciated, and she replied, without hesitation, "Accumulating money."

I call Schwartz on the phone from time to time, and, as a conversation opener, often say, "How're you doing?" "Oh, all right," he has responded on more than one occasion. "I made seven or eight grand last week."

Traders and brokers commingle about the heating-oil ring—the mobocracy that will have a lot to say about whether the price of future heating-oil deliveries will be higher or lower this day. Last-minute arrivals are forced to set up for business on the very outer fringes of the trading area: the good spots are gone. Murderous intent already flickers on some faces—no doubt those of traders who got creamed yesterday. There is the usual pre–trading-bell salacious banter. "Check out this curvy clerk. Wouldn't you like to fill up her tank with some heating oil?" Squeezing into the circle and leaning over the shoulder of another trader, Schwartz calls out, "Hey, give me some stationery, huh." The clerk squatting in the center of the ring hands him a pile of index-sized cards. Once again, Schwartz will invest not a cent of his own money in paper supplies.

"What do you hear, kid?" Schwartz inquires of a heating-oil diehard standing next to him.

"I hear it's like duck soup outside," he replies.

"What's that got to do with heating oil?"

"What do I know? Ask the guy in the boiler room. He'd know more about heating oil than I would."

A bell rings. A blue-smocked official, trying to muffle a hacking cough, raps a hammer three times and calls off the first contract month. Trading begins with "Call," meaning that lots are sold by the month in sequential fashion until there's no more interest; then the trading is opened to any bids for any month. Heating-oil trading continues until 2:45. The commodity is limited to a two-cent-per-gallon swing. The smallest contract that can be traded is forty-three thousand gallons. Each two-cent fluctuation can earn or lose a trader a total of eight hundred and sixty dollars.

Schwartz quickly makes a fistful of trades in an effort to disentangle himself from an adverse position he got himself into yesterday. He steps back for a moment, runs his hand along his scalp, and consults his scribblings. His expression becomes quizzical. "They had me on the opening. I was short, and the price was up. I'm trading around my position. Let's see; I sold twenty-nine lots and I bought twenty-nine lots. I'm still short." Stimulated, he dashes back into the frenzy. For the next half-hour, he is a perpetual-motion machine, shifting, swaying, bobbing, weaving, reaching.

As a personal rule, Schwartz tries to worm his way into a spot adjacent to a commission broker. "It's better than standing next to a trader," he says, "because a broker has public orders and the public are assholes. So who would you rather trade with—assholes or a trader? The public is always losing money. The public shouldn't be in this business. Why should someone let you make money at their own game?"

"Anyone else you like to be near?" I ask.

"Yeah, some guys are good indicators."

"Indicators of what?"

"They're always wrong. With some guys, I have parties

every time they trade. Some guys shouldn't be down here. They have limited bank rolls and so they're scared money. You shouldn't trade with scared money. If you trade with scared money, you don't have two guesses. If you're wrong on the first guess, you're gone. Bye-bye."

"Forty-five for November. Forty-five for November. Forty-five for November." Schwartz is bidding 95.45¢ per gallon for a lot of November heating oil.

Nobody bites. A man to Schwartz's right, however, offers an October lot for twenty-five, and Schwartz says, "I'll buy it." He jots down the purchase on a card.

That trade done, Schwartz tries again with November. "Forty-five for November. Forty-five for November. Forty-five for November."

The cries go for naught, so he switches months. "Seventy-five for December. Seventy-five for December. Seventy-five for December."

Not having much success with winter, he pushes on to spring. "Fifteen for March. Fifteen for March. Fifteen for March." (Here, a gallon is selling for $100.15.)

He picks up some Marches from a hooknosed trader to his left, then retreats to cooler months. "Seventy-five for November. Seventy-five for November." Before he shouts it out again, he catches himself, realizing that he is stating his December bid for November, an absurdly high price. A broker to his right yells, "Take 'em."

"Wait a minute, I meant seventy-five for December," Schwartz says.

"You said seventy-five for November."

"I lied." Schwartz shrugs. "I lied. I don't have to tell the truth." Schwartz will be chivalrous on occasion but not foolhardy.

As bids fill the air, Schwartz's head rocks from side to side. He nods here to acknowledge acceptance of a bid. He nods there to consent to a sale. Sometimes, he begins a nod in one direction, then abruptly reverses rocks and nods elsewhere to take advantage of a riper opportunity. "Warren's got the best head fake since Elgin Baylor," I have been told by one of his colleagues.

His visual coverage of the ring is hindered slightly by the fact that his left eye is plastic. The real eye never matured after he was born, and doctors removed it when he was three. When I asked him if his eyesight put him at any disadvantage, he said, "Don't forget, a good trader can hear everything. I hear like I've got four ears." He went on to cite some personal precautions he has adopted. "I make sure that when I trade with somebody, he knows I'm looking at him. I yell 'I sold it to you' and scream his name. Otherwise, a guy may be looking at my plastic eye and think I'm trading with him and I'm not. Another thing I do is, I hit a guy on the shoulder if I want to trade with him. They don't like that too much. But I keep doing it. Let me ask you something. If it costs you five thousand dollars not to hit someone on the shoulder, do you do it?"

A few years ago, Schwartz used to abide by a back-breaking schedule. His routine was to trade cocoa from 9:30 to 10:00 A.M. and sugar from 10:00 to 1:00; then he would dash over to the American Stock Exchange and trade options from 1:15 to 4:00. "I had to be at every casino in town," he recalls. Finally, one night he had a seizure. He didn't heed the warning, and a month later he suffered a second, more severe, seizure that caused his left shoulder to separate. Doctors were unable to isolate a cause, but Schwartz figured he knew the answer. "It had to be the mental pressure," he says. "Physically, I was okay. I thrive on the physical stuff. It was the pressure of running to all those tables, making all those decisions." Thus he decided that he'd better limit his adventures to one floor. Even during his recovery period, though, when his left arm hung in a sling for six weeks, Schwartz refused to sink into a life of indolence. He kept reporting to the rings. About the only pity he got from fellow traders was the offer of a stool to sit on at the American Exchange. "It was painful, walking around in a sling, holding a pad with my bad arm and writing with my other arm," he recalls. "I got the shit kicked out of me in the rings. I couldn't even trade in the rings. I was getting beaten and pushed. I had to stand on the outside. The doctor had asked me if having a seizure at work would affect my business. No, I said. The other guys would step right over me. They wouldn't stop trading. And it's true. They wouldn't stop trading if there was a dead moose lying in the ring."

Trading continues at a frenzied clip. A man with a salt-and-pepper beard and bifocals is trading as if his days are numbered—and, depending on the contents of his wallet, perhaps they are. Also working hard is a fat man whose badge identification is MAIN. Other badges in the crowd read: ZZ, TEA, JADE, SNOW, HILL, CASH, CAT, GAS, COZY, BUBY, RGEE, and, most aptly, OIL. Schwartz's badge just sports his initials—WMS.

Some months elicit little more than a yawn from the jumble of traders. Others all but touch off fisticuffs. At one point, in fact, a trader slyly sells another trader a May contract at a clearly unfavorable price. The inflamed buyer thought he meant a different month. The seller refuses to "break" the trade. Shaking with rage, the sucker marches over to the trader and socks him in the jaw. The two quickly sink into a full-fledged fistfight, punishing clips flying back and forth, until exchange officials intercede and bust it up. Both men get slapped with fines. Watching the occasional brutality of the trading, I muse that it would not be a bad idea to institute a penalty box, much like the kind used in professional hockey, so that if a deviant trader is spied elbowing a colleague or checking him in the chin with his deck of cards, he will be shuttled into the penalty box for two to five minutes (depending on whether he has drawn blood), where he will sit cringing, watching profit opportunities slip away, positions deteriorate hopelessly.

"Emotions tend to run pretty strong down here," Schwartz informs me dryly in the wake of the fight. Unfazed, he zips back into the ring to pick up a couple of December lots and to unload some Novembers.

The fury of the opening over, traders start to drift from the ring. New ones sidle over, but the activity begins to wane. "What's going on here?" Schwartz declares. "Do they know we're open?"

During the lull, I take my notebook with me and roam about the floor.

Ed Moritt, silver trader, is sprawling across the wooden railing of the monstrous silver pit, his left foot off the ground, his right foot on tiptoe, his right arm outstretched, as if he were reaching over the side of a boat in the hope of rescuing a swimmer going under for the third time. As it happens, he is trying to get hold of some Marches being offered by a man across the ring.

Moritt is a strapping, good-looking man in his early forties, with an infectious air of derring-do about him. He grew up in Brooklyn, where his father ran a prosperous plumbing-and heating-supply business. He went to college in Miami with the anticipation of going into law, but got sidetracked and caught the trading bug when he started accompanying his roommate to a local brokerage house. Moritt was infatuated with the video displays that unendingly show the prices going up and down. After college, he worked as a broker and then a branch manager at several Miami firms, before he finally realized his dream and bought a seat on the New York Stock Exchange. After a year as a floor broker, he started trading strictly for himself.

Moritt is the type who can never get enough. Thus, while he traded stocks, he also took fliers in the commodity markets. In the spring of 1973, his moonlighting caught up with him in a particularly vicious way. At the time, Moritt was short a great many soybeans (he is embarrassed to bandy the number) when the soybean market erupted in one of its greatest upward swings ever. Moritt had sold the beans for something like four to four and a half dollars per bushel. For two straight weeks, watching in terror as the price of soybeans rocketed higher, he was unable to get out of the market. There were no sellers, only buyers. Beans hit twelve dollars a bushel by the time Moritt was finally able to cover his positions. He reckons he dropped roughly forty thousand dollars per lot of soybeans. In short, Moritt was wiped out. He had lost more money than he had. Prudence might have suggested the somber solution of personal bankruptcy, but Moritt was not about to be prudent now. "I didn't want to go bankrupt," he tells me. "It would have been much easier, but I never considered it because of the way I would have felt about myself. Not to pay off my debt when I was fully able to just didn't sit well with me." The money was owed to two brokerage houses, and so, swallowing hard, Moritt abandoned trading for himself and undertook commission work for them.

He had already sold a sumptuous house in Connecticut and replaced it with a more modest dwelling in Westchester. He also disposed of his collections of artwork and antique cars. On the floor of the stock exchange, he worked like a possessed man. He racked up fees of thirty to fifty thousand dollars a month, a herculean amount of work. "I did the work of ten men," Moritt recalls. "I never worked so hard in my life. I was like Paul Bunyan." By day's end, he was spent, and barely mustered the energy to catch his train home. Out of his big earnings, though, he saw nothing. All of the proceeds went to pay off his indebtedness. For walking-around money, Moritt borrowed from his brother, who was in the textile business in Minneapolis. It was not until the very end of 1976 that Moritt was a free man again, his debt finally gone. He left the stock exchange to try his luck at commodities full-time, and after flirtations in Chicago and also on the options exchange, he found his way to silver, where he's enjoyed his greatest success. Now, he restricts his risk-taking exclusively to silver. "I learned you should trade where you are and not where you have no control. If I had been there in the soybean pit, it wouldn't have happened. I would have anticipated it." Despite his almost ruinous experience, though, Moritt has not seen fit to invest any of his leftover funds in safer nests. He still prefers to lay it on the line daily. "I think the best way to live is to just get through today and tomorrow and not worry about the future."

Not that the experience has been fully expunged from his memory. Once I spoke with Moritt on the phone and I asked him how traders deal with the heavy risks. "They deal with themselves," he said. "It's the hardest thing to deal with. I had a big losing day today. It's very easy to lose respect for yourself. It's a very, very difficult life. It's very easy, when you keep losing, to say to yourself, What am I doing in such an irresponsible life-style? It's very hard when you lose and you have a lot of people depending on you."

Now, Moritt gazes at the silver ring. "It's a very difficult life. It's not easy at all. If it were easy, they'd be lined up to do it."

Almost noon. Schwartz turns to me and says, "Look at this. It's dead. Nothing's doing. This is what happens in the middle of the day." He fiddles with his cards. The lack of bids has induced a dreamy lethargy in him. Also, hunger pangs have set in. Some energetic traders, bored when the activity subsides in the afternoon, wrap up their positions, shuck their trading smocks, and take off for the local horse tracks. They get their afternoon fix there.

"If nothing happens in the next few minutes," Schwartz finally says, "then forget it, we'll go to lunch."

The exchange cafeteria is a smallish place of modern decor that resembles a *nouveau chic* eatery. About half of the tables are occupied. One beaverish man is working on some charts while wrestling with an overstuffed turkey club. At a nearby table, a man and a young woman are deep in hushed conversation. One suspects a Tahiti fling or some such thing, but, no, the lackluster nature of the sugar market is what's on their mind.

With characteristic dispatch, Schwartz grabs some chicken soup, a piece of apple pie, a pint of milk, and a cup of tea. He tells the cashier, "I'm long soup, pie, tea, and milk. I'm short money." He draws not even a smirk, and we slip into black-cushioned chairs at a large table with two other traders, who have lately been working the coffee ring. The younger of the two seems awfully sullen, which is explained later when he happens to mention that he has dropped about thirty grand in the past week. Traders find great fun in ribbing one another, and before he has slurped halfway through his soup, Schwartz becomes the target of their jibes. The elder trader says, "Warren's sight is so bad he's like the blind guy who goes by the fish market and says, 'Good morning, girls.'"

The tablemate says, "I've seen Warren say good morning to a telephone pole."

"I probably have," Schwartz says.

Schwartz and I start talking about the amount of research (or, more likely, the dearth of it) that traders do. What do you know about heating oil? I ask.

"I wouldn't know heating oil if it stood me in the face," he replies. "I wouldn't know heating oil if I swam it. The less you know, the better off you are. If you know too much, you start getting an opinion, and then they throw you out the window. If you have an opinion, then you're basically trading the market. It's much better not to have an opinion."

To confirm his point, Schwartz grabs the sleeve of one of our tablemates and asks him, "Tell me, you ever do any research?"

"Yeah, I tried it once," he says with a bit of a sneer.

"How much did you lose?" Schwartz asks.

"Plenty. It doesn't pay to think. Most people here, they don't think. They react."

A trader at the next table spies Schwartz and calls over, "Hey, Warren, why don't you come over to the green pit?" The man is a silver trader.

"You know me," Schwartz says, shaking his head. "I'm not like you. I'm too cautious. I wipe the toilet seat three times before I go."

Schwartz spoons a mountain of sugar into his tea and says to me, "He's a shooter. He's back and forth fifty thousand dollars a day. Some guys are outright shooters. They bet on the market. They're like degenerate gamblers. They lose a million, they make a million. Some guys are real players, real big shooters. The guy behind you, he bets five hundred dollars on a basketball game. If I had his guts, I'd make a fortune."

Schwartz shovels in a helping of pie, takes a swig of milk, then says, "A lot of guys come to me down here and say they want to start and learn the business, what can they make? Without killing yourself, I tell them, you ought to make two hundred dollars a day. It goes up from there."

Schwartz is somewhat more open-minded than many of his colleagues about unorthodox ways of getting ahead in the trading game, and, after bolting down a few more mouthfuls of pie, he tells me his sunspot episode:

"I met this guy from Chicago who was a tennis bum. He used to play tennis all the time and hustle people. He had this system of trading options and commodities by sunspots. He came and talked to me one day and I listened to him and I said, Okay, let's try it. I put him on retainer for three hundred dollars a week, and he was supposed to tell me what to do. I was trading options then on the American Stock Exchange. So he says Aquarius is in tune with Mars and some cockamamie story, and he says the market has to come down. I put in some spreads and all and the market collapses and I made a ton of money. Then he says, Don't do anything for a couple of weeks. The market has to come down. I do it and I make money. One day, at two in the afternoon, he says there was a total eclipse and the market's going to come down. The market was up like seven points and it wasn't coming down. I said, Aquarius, where are you, and it started to come down and I made a lot of money. Finally, he had some bad days and I was getting nervous with him. He started to use his head and look at what the market was doing, and if he saw it was down for four days, he'd say it had to go up. Once he started using his head, he was no good, so I got rid of him. But I made a lot of money with him. I kept him about three months and I did all right."

Schwartz chuckles at the memory of the episode and slurps some tea.

Schwartz was born and reared in Teaneck, New Jersey. His father was a lawyer, and Schwartz was instilled early with the belief that, if he wanted to get anywhere worthwhile in the world, he had to become a professional man. One of his aunts, however, was addicted to the stock market in the way that other middle-aged women are smitten with needlepoint. "Every time I went to see her, she was in her brokerage house," Schwartz recalls. "She couldn't pass a brokerage house without going in. When I was eight years old, she used to drag me with her to the broker, and so by the time I was twelve I was looking at stock tables in the paper." After a short stint of regularly studying the columns of numbers that made up the tables, Schwartz was ready to give the market a fling. Seeing what for now obscure reasons seemed to him a sure-fire opportunity to make his fortune early, he scrounged together ten dollars and sank it into five shares of Webber Knapp, a real-estate concern that has since ingloriously collapsed into bankruptcy. On its way to ruin, it took Schwartz's money with it. "So I lost money like everyone else, but I got involved." When he reached the more investment-savvy age of fourteen, Schwartz smelled paydirt in a different stock and snapped up some shares of Israel Mediterranean Petroleum. Its price rose like a bird from two dollars to seven. Today it, too, lies buried in the corporate graveyard.

"When I was in high school," Schwartz recounts, "I got my parents into the market. They lost money. And, I'll tell you, that was the best thing that ever happened to me. Know why? Because I realized that the average guy shouldn't be in the market. The commissions are too high and he doesn't know enough. The edge is against him. This, incidentally, may have given me my cynical attitude. I started to look around and I realized what greed does to people. Greed makes people do things they shouldn't do. I realized that you have to make money in your own business. That's the key to life. You have to stay within your own realm. You have to do what you know you can do."

Schwartz was a miserable student in high school. He failed algebra and didn't perform much better in other subjects. All told, 527 students graduated in his class; Schwartz ranked a lowly 487th. When asked to appraise his intellectual prowess, Schwartz will respond waggishly, "I would consider myself a dumb Jew." His choices of higher education restricted by his rotten academic standing, he opted to attend the undistinguished Rider College in undistinguished Trenton. Even to get admitted there, he recalls, he had to pull some strings with a person of some influence in Trenton. He studied finance, with the vague aspiration of becoming an accountant. Quickly, however, he found himself immersed in a life of unending gambling. Tuesdays, Wednesdays, and Thursdays, it was relatively easy to track down Schwartz's whereabouts. He could be found at the bettors' windows at Garden State Park, a nearby horse track. It became his custom to stay up until two in the morning in his apartment studying *Turf and Track Digest*, making his picks. Nothing short of a severe cash-flow problem would keep Schwartz from the betting windows, and sometimes not even that would interfere. "There was this one day when I had no money at all. I was flat broke. So, you know, I see they're giving away twenty-five dollars to give blood. Why not? I figure. So two of my friends drive me to the hospital and I get in there and I'm pumping away, really going strong, but the needle is in wrong and the blood is just dribbling out and I've got to make the Daily Double. I say to the nurse, Put the needle in the other arm, I've got to make the Daily Double. She says to keep pumping. So I pump and pump and they finally get three-quarters of a bottle of blood and they hand me my twenty-five bucks. I'm running short of time, and so my two friends carry me down the stairs, because I'm a little dizzy. They open up all the windows in the car and they say, Start picking, because I was a pretty good picker. You know the way the teachers post grades on sheets in the hallways? One guy put up a sheet that had 'Handicapping One' and 'Handicapping Two.' I always used to get an A in Handicapping One and Two. So I make my picks, we finally get to the track, and I lose my money after five races and we go home."

After a while, Schwartz's interest in the ponies dwindled, and he began betting sports. At first, he toyed with professional events but quickly soured on them. "I stopped betting pro sports because I thought they were fixed. With basketball, it's all in the last two minutes. I also realized that the difference between the best and the worst is only ten percent. You know, if the difference between the best and the worst is only ten percent, you don't have the edge." Migrating to college football and basketball, Schwartz developed a theory that his odds were most advantageous if, after carefully researching the teams of games to be contested in a given week, he chose just one and bet heavily on it. His research habits would impress a Harvard historian. "I would keep old copies of the *Times* that had the reports of the games. I would make up my own charts. I would call up the athletic departments of out-of-town schools to see if anyone was hurt and I'd even check what the weather forecast was like. Weather matters, you know. I made a rule that I would only bet teams in the East, and I would only bet a team if I could visit it and see it play or, as a fallback, if I could listen to a game on the radio, so I'd have an idea of what the defenses and offenses were like. I had it down almost to a science. Most of the time, I would bet twenty-five dollars, sometimes a hundred. The bet was usually even money and I'd win most of the time. It was good money back then. This was in the early sixties, and I was making twenty-five to a hundred bucks a week. That was nothing to complain about."

Schwartz's proclivity for gambling rather than tackling his schoolwork made for some odd exchanges with his parents. "When I came home from school and my mother would ask me how I did in school, I said I had made a hundred dollars or I had made sixty dollars. I was the only student who, when my mother asked me how I did, said I made money or I lost money."

After he graduated from college, Schwartz found a job as a margin clerk at the New York brokerage house of Spingarn, Heine & Company. He was told he would be promoted to trader within six months' time, but it never happened. "They fired me after six months because they saw I was interested in fourteen other things and that I was too aggressive." Next, he tried his hand at accounting. He bounced from firm to firm. He quit one company of his own volition, since the regimen of the place caused his interest to flag rapidly. A second institution fired him after he tore a ligament in his leg while water-skiing: the firm got fed up with his protracted absence. He joined yet a third accounting company, saw himself going nowhere, and departed after nine months of wearing their eyeshades. Jaded with puzzling out people's taxes, Schwartz bounded back into the stock-brokerage business, where he proceeded to make a further horror out of his résumé. He settled in as a broker at Weiss, Weiss, Voisin and Cannon and left after a year. He joined Charles Plohn and Company. A year later, he was fired. He tells the specifics best: "The market was falling apart and I saw what kind of deals they were doing, all these new, risky issues. So I got up in the middle of the office one day and said that everyone was going to lose their job because the firm was going to go out of business in a year. I was always one to say what I thought. My prediction didn't quite endear me with the boss, and so I was fired. Incidentally, I was wrong. The firm went bankrupt in six months." Schwartz packed up and tried Filor Bullard and Smyth, where he was again fired after a year. (Forces conspired against Schwartz with such regularity that it was beginning to seem as if a papal decree had been issued to the effect that Warren Schwartz was to be canned from whatever job he held after a maximum of a year's service.) This time, it was because Schwartz was spending the greater part of his time moon-lighting on the floor of the New York Stock Exchange, trying to drum up business for himself. "The way my luck was running, if I had bought artificial flowers, they would have died," Schwartz says.

After collecting unemployment for a while and beginning to wonder if he were going to have to take up the tin-cup routine, he arranged to join the firm of Phillip Budin, only to watch in horror as it went belly-up before he even had a chance to report for work. Then he became a partner at Austin James & Company, with the usual sequel: "I was on vacation and they were convinced that there was something wrong with this stock I was trading. So they sold it all while I was away and took a fifteen-thousand-dollar bath. They tried to sue me. In fact, they did sue me. I refused to pay and they fired me." Dishy, Easton & Company took on the peripatetic Schwartz next, and he evinces some pride in the fact that they didn't fire him. While there, he boned up on the rudiments of the commodities business. He was targeted to become a floor trader for Dishy, but the litigation against him muddled things. All of this was causing a certain amount of pain to Schwartz. "I finally decided to start doing things on my own. I developed a floor-trading brokerage at the Mercantile Exchange. I was incompetent. The first year I had fifteen thousand dollars' worth of errors on seventy-five thousand dollars of brokerage. Absolutely pathetic. I didn't know what the hell I was doing. I was a man in a raft without oars. The answer is, I was incompetent."

He stuck it out for a year and a half, then bought an options seat on the American Stock Exchange. The rules then stipulated that you had to have ready capital of seventy-five thousand dollars to become a bona-fide floor trader. Schwartz argued vehemently that that was too much, in large part because he was not nearly flush enough and had no way of scaring up that kind of money. The Amex was unyielding, and so the pluckily independent Schwartz traded off the floor until the exchange, drawing little interest in its seats, finally caved in and relaxed the capital requirement to twenty-five thousand. Armed with sixteen thousand dollars in cash and a ten-thousand-dollar Treasury bill, Schwartz moved onto the floor to try to prove his mettle in the rough-and-tumble world of floor trading.

This was 1974. He had found his niche. Since then, he has been regularly netting gratifying sums of money. "I think I made a hundred thousand dollars the first year. Every year from then on, I always made at least a hundred thousand dollars." After a couple of years of options trading, Schwartz moved to commodities, where he sniffed still bigger money, and apart from occasional flings with options and stocks, he's traded commodities ever since.

Given that Schwartz is fanatically attentive to making money, his attitude toward adversity, which he has had his share of despite his string of winning years, might be described as the cowardice theory. "When I'm wrong, I run," Schwartz tells me when I ask him to explain the theory to me. "Listen, when I'm wrong, I sell my seat and run like hell. I bought a sugar seat once. The first week I'm there, I have errors like crazy. I had a new kid, green as a Martian, writing up my orders for me, and he's making mistakes like there's a reward for them. They fined me a thousand dollars for errors. On top of that, I was losing money. I was making a hundred and fifty thousand at the Amex and here I'm losing money. I called up the Amex and bought my seat back. I'm ready to sell the sugar seat, but I say, Ah, I'll wait a week. I started making money like crazy so I stayed. But I've run before. Eight years ago, at the Merc, I saw a market start to die—I was trading platinum and potatoes—and so I sold my seat for ten thousand dollars, after I paid seventeen. I started losing money and there was no liquidity. I didn't like what I saw, so I ran. When I'm going bad, I'll stop trading for several days or I'll bet dollars. When I used to bet sports, I would bet fifty cents when I was going bad."

Since moving to the commodity rings, Schwartz could immerse himself in the trappings of a millionaire. Yet success has worked few changes in his life-style. He lives in a very nice but not ostentatious condominium and on weekends he lives in not too much country splendor in a small house built for little money in Southampton, Long Island. (Summers, he knocks off on Fridays and Mondays to spend more time on the tennis courts and beaches, becoming a three-day-a-week trader.) One of his few concessions is the silver Mercedes he drives, having graduated a few years ago from a Chevette. Practicality, however, sparked the switch: after suffering his seizure, Schwartz was concerned about being stricken while he was driving, and so he wanted to improve his odds with one of the sturdiest vehicles on the road. "I couldn't care less otherwise. It's a car. A Mercedes, a Chevette— they're cars."

Schwartz can be prudent almost to a fault. Once, when he had invited me over to dinner at his Southampton place, he served lobster. Lobster, of course, can be gotten at any of a dozen nearby fish markets. But Schwartz chose a market in New Jersey, where he also picked up the vegetables and other accoutrements. The prices, he explained, were much better. "People ask me why don't I live like a millionaire," Schwartz will say when the question of living up to one's means comes up. "They come over to my house and they say, Why aren't you in some big digs down on the water? Listen, if I lived like a millionaire I wouldn't be a millionaire. You don't got it unless you got it."

Trading is a very masculine game. It has some of the over-tones of a football locker room. Women are so rare among the traders that you specifically notice them. The Board of Trade first allowed women on its floor only in 1969; it was 1978 before the New York Coffee and Sugar Exchange admitted a woman. Female runners are in fair abundance nowadays, but women traders are still a scarcity. No more than a half-dozen or so have seats on the Comex. Many men traders im-plicitly—or explicitly—suggest that women have abjured the profession because they just don't have the constitution or the guts to play a game that would test the mettle of even the Bionic Woman, but some women seem to get by and are indulged. I have wondered what it is like for a woman in the mad scuffles of the commodity wilds, and one morning I talk with Cindy Cray about it. She is a nice-looking, cherub-faced woman in her late twenties. Her brown hair is worn at above-shoulder length. She has a sparkling manner, a direct, point-blank regard, and the rosy cheeks of someone who is doing well. She is wearing a well-creased lime skirt and a striped blouse. Other traders have told me she is a shrewd, hard-driving woman, full of ambition. Part of a firm called NCZ Commodities, she does trading for customer accounts as well as for herself. For the most part, she says, she rummages around the gold ring, the most hectic on the floor.

She informs me that she was educated at Smith. Her majors were math and economics. "In school, I didn't know what I wanted to do, to be honest with you." Her first job was at Bloomingdale's. "I was in the management-training program. It was too slow and too boring. You had to do basic grunt work—pick out clothes and all that. I stayed six months." Her father was a stockbroker, so there was a little trading in her manner and her soul. A buddy working at NCZ told her there was an opening, and she walked in and landed the job, seeing it as an escape from the clothes racks. She started out trading stocks off the floor, moved into commodities, and for the last eighteen months has been down on the floor, working the rings. The first time she toured the trading floor of a commodity exchange, she thought to herself, "You really had to have empty room upstairs to be down here." Once exposed, though, she wanted to trade.

"What is it like out there for a woman?" I ask her.

"I get tossed and bumped and yelled at like everyone else," she says. "You get bashed around. But I push and shove like the next guy. In terms of my bids, they're just as good as anyone else's. I may have difficulty getting my bids executed, but that's a factor of the market, not my sex. I have a big advantage in my voice. I have a very piercing, loud voice. And it never gives out. Some women have a problem in that their voices are too soft. Their bids don't get heard. In fact, I get teased about my voice. The guys in the ring try to mimic it. That's great! Then more traders know what I'm trying to do."

"The teasing doesn't bother you?"

She fixes me with a hawklike stare and says, "I have three younger brothers and three young stepbrothers. So, believe me, I'm used to being teased. In fact, I would think there'd be something wrong if they didn't tease me. You wouldn't be part of the gang. I tease them back. If someone's voice cracks, I'll ask them if they're trying to imitate me. If someone has on a shirt and tie that clash, they'll hear about it from me."

"How's your stamina?"

"I've always had a lot of jobs during the summers standing on my feet. I was on my feet all day at Bloomingdale's. But I'm exhausted all right at the end of the day. Many Friday nights I'll go home and go to bed at nine o'clock, I'm so tired from the week."

I wonder if she is ever abused by some of the hotheaded men.

"I've never had anyone try to physically abuse me," she says. "If I'm in the way, they'll try to move me away just like anyone else. Sometimes, someone will step on my foot. *I* may step on someone's foot, too. I bruise very easily. Some days, I'll come home and have black-and-blues on my arm. It's just part of this business."

She laughs delightedly, and then adds, "One day there were twenty seconds left to the close in gold and I had to get in there. I just had to get in the ring. I literally threw two people out of the ring. I apologized afterward, but I had no choice. I had to get in there."

Then she peeks at her watch, pats down her skirt, smiles warmly, and says that she is sorry but the gold market is opening in fifteen minutes; she beats a hasty retreat.

Arms sawing the air, Schwartz is trading cocoa. He looks glum. For three straight days, he's been murdered in cocoa. He doesn't want to know about cocoa. If someone were to offer him a Hershey bar he might blanch. What's more, he has the beginnings of a sore throat, a malady as hazardous to a commodity trader as it is to Luciano Pavarotti. He is sucking lozenges, trying to nurse his throat through a few more hours.

Cocoa talk: "March at sixty . . . March at sixty-five . . . Sell two . . . Eighty-one for Deece . . . March at sixty . . . Take two March at sixty . . . Sold two . . . Who sold me one March at sixty? . . . Deece five . . . Now, what did I just get here at sixty . . . Maaaarch, three for two . . . Deece at five . . . Deece at eighty, Deece at eighty . . . Seventy-seven for ten Deece, who wants it . . . Eighty . . . Take it . . . Twenty-three for July . . . Forty-nine for September . . . Eighty-five for Deece . . . Buy ten . . . Hey, Kenny, Deece at eighty-five . . . Now, who'd I buy it from? I bought ten and ten . . . March at seventy, March at seventy, March at sixty-eight . . . I'll give you a quarter for eleven Julys . . . Eighty-five for six Deece is all I want . . . Eighty-five for six Deece is all I want . . . Ten July . . . March at sixty-five . . . Offered at sixty-seven, Tommy, best bid is five . . . Two Deece at ninety . . . Aldo, what's your number . . . Four fucking twenty-two . . . Okay,

four fucking twenty-two . . . Eighty-five for Deece, five bid
. . . March at sixty-five . . . Deece at eighty-five . . . I'll buy
ten. No, I won't buy ten. I'll buy—yeah, I'll buy ten. . . ."

Today, as it happens, is Schwartz's birthday. Some years
ago, when he was trading on the American Stock Exchange,
his friends marked the occasion by shoving a pie in his face.
"They called me over into a crowd and some guys held me
and they threw a pie in my face," Schwartz recalls. "It was a
lemon meringue. The pity is, I don't even like lemon
meringue."

Having his fill of cocoa, Schwartz goes over to the heating-
oil ring. Heating oil opens up. Then down. Then up. It's
what traders call a "whipsaw market." Schwartz is, for the
most part, docile, picking up a few crumbs here and there.
He noses over the bids and offers, like a mouse checking out
some cheese. Bored by the pace after a while, he shuffles
over to a video terminal and punches some buttons to see
how the stock market is doing. Then he races to a phone,
calls a broker, and buys five hundred shares of Digital
Equipment.

"Why'd you buy the Digital Equipment?" I ask, sifting for
some glimmer of market intelligence.

"I don't know." Schwartz shrugs. "I just saw it there."

He smacks his forehead. Some spreads have moved to
prices that practically scream for him to sell and pocket the
profits. He lunges into the ring, wagging his fingers, gets rid
of five contracts. Calmed down, he licks his thumb, as if tast-
ing the money he just made.

"Can you move the market, Warren?" I ask.

"Sure. You can do it for twenty minutes. You can do it for a
half-hour. But nobody's got the money to affect the market
for long. The market's going where it's going. Listen, you got

cancer. You can deter it. You can postpone it. But you got cancer, you know what, you're going to die."

Now Schwartz is betting gasoline. In between trades, a broker is talking to him about acoustics. "At the gold ring, the acoustics are so bad you can't hear twenty feet away from you," the broker says.

Schwartz says, "I was in heating oil once and this guy was trading right and left. I couldn't hear a thing. I wondered if I was a dumb Jew."

A trader across the ring gives Schwartz a woebegone look. He has helped Schwartz out of tight squeezes in the past.

"You hurting?" Schwartz asks. "You need help?"

"I'm getting creamed," the trader says. "The hearse is going to be here soon."

"Here, I'll sell you a November at eighty."

Schwartz retreats to the phones. He calls the Amex and puts on some option spreads. He phones the New York Stock Exchange and buys some stock. He's got to get his fix somewhere.

He returns to the ring, where the crowd is getting restless. "What do I got to do, buy you dinner to sell," a hirsute trader in a short-sleeved shirt howls.

"Yeah," Schwartz yells back. "I want a steak dinner, baked potato, and salad bar. Then I'll buy."

"The guy's bagged," Schwartz whispers to me. "He's got four lots and he can't get rid of them. It's like he's got leprosy or the plague. So he wants someone to bail him out."

"This fucking market," the hirsute trader stammers. "It sucks." He stomps off, his face set in a rancorous scowl, cursing to himself.

Schwartz stands in the ring now, looking like an awestruck kid at his first amusement park, wondering which ride to try first. He studies the price board, studies the faces of the other traders, peers at his trading cards. He swings his gaze back up to the board, gnaws at a thumbnail, wonders: Take a November? Sell some Deeces? Hmmm. Sounds interesting. But who knows? He pauses, arches his neck. He looks tired. He remains inert. "Ah," he says. "How much money can you make?"

Then Schwartz steps out of the ring. He smiles, leans back, and sighs, secure and contented, and watches the other traders groping for money.

INDEX